GROWING
HERBS

FROM SEED, CUTTING & ROOT

GROWING

An adventure in small miracles

HERBS

FROM SEED, CUTTING & ROOT

THOMAS DEBAGGIO

 INTERWEAVE PRESS

Growing Herbs from Seed, Cutting & Root
An Adventure in Small Miracles
by Thomas DeBaggio

Design, Signorella Graphic Arts
Photography, Joe Coca, except pages 17, 18, and 35
Production, Marc McCoy Owens

Interweave Press, Inc.
201 East Fourth Street
Loveland, Colorado 80537
USA

Printed in the United States of America

Library of Congress Cataloging-in-Publication Data

DeBaggio, Thomas, 1942–
    Growing herbs from seed, cutting & root : an adventure in small
miracles / Thomas DeBaggio.
        p.   cm.
    Includes index.
    ISBN 0-934026-96-3 : $9.95
    1. Herb gardening.   2. Herbs.   3. Container gardening.   I. Title.
SB351.H5D43   1994
635'.7—dc20
                                                    94-38609
                                                    CIP

First printing: IWP—20M:1194:QUE

To my son, Francesco,

who sacrificed the best afternoons of his youth

so I could pursue my dream to grow herbs on what he

thought would be his backyard soccer field.

FOREWORD

Gardening is a hopeful pursuit. Its ultimate end may be the showy display, the bountiful harvest, but its first joys are in optimistic beginnings. Marvelling at the tiny, stout, pebbled seed leaves of a common garden sage, rejoicing at the appearance of pale, translucent nubs of root on the nodes of a scented geranium cutting, watching a favorite lavender leapfrog through the flower border by successful layering—these are among the richest rewards of herb gardening.

Good beginnings don't come easy, though. Seeds languish, seedlings grow lanky and succumb to disease, cuttings rot, divisions fail to thrive. Besides luck, success requires knowledge, experience, perseverance, the ability to think like a plant. Tom DeBaggio has developed these qualities in abundance during his twenty-five years of working with herbs.

Growing Herbs from Seed, Cutting, and Root collects the insights, experiences, techniques, and trade secrets he has accrued during those years, and he shares them here with generosity and a grain of salt. You'll find conventional wisdom spelled out in a fresh new way, unorthodox approaches that make perfect sense, and an enthusiasm for the miracles of growth that can carry you through a lifetime of rewarding seasons in the garden.

Linda Ligon
editor, *The Herb Companion*

PREFACE

This book will tell you, and more important, show you, some of the tricks I've developed for producing large, vigorous, and healthy herbs. I've come by these techniques honestly; I worked hard for them.

After twenty-five years as a home gardener, I decided two decades ago to grow plants for a living. Herb plants in garden centers, when they could be found then, didn't compare to the gorgeous bedding and vegetable plants by their sides; they had a tragic look to them. Why didn't herbs look better? The answer was simple: they weren't grown with the same skill and care as bedding plants. There were no books for commercial growers of herbs then, so I began experimenting, and over the years I've come up with a number of innovative ways to grow herb plants.

Thousands of customers and hundreds of thousands of plants have taught me many things about the herb garden. One of the most important lessons I learned early: gardening isn't only about plants; it's also about time. Contrary to what many gardeners believe, the most important time for a plant is before a seedling germinates or a cutting roots. Seeds await their season of fulfillment, which is unlocked by the gardener who has a clear sense of time. After the two weeks or so in which a viable seed becomes a healthy, promising seedling (or a thick, vigorous stem-tip becomes a well-rooted cutting), the next most important time is the eight weeks that follow germination or rooting. This is the formative time in the tender world of plants and the most difficult for the home gardener to control; but anybody with some spare space, a little commitment, and the enthusiasm to closely observe nature's unfolding process can produce herb transplants to rival a professional.

While the first ten or twelve weeks in an herb's life are the most critical to its later performance, and are the focus of this book, there are a few tips at the end about transplanting, spacing, and pruning that will get you through the remainder of the season with healthy, bountiful plants.

There are as many reasons to grow your own herbs as there are ways to grow healthy plants, but the main reasons for me are that it's fun, simple, and you get to watch small miracles happen; it's the most satisfying part of herb gardening—next to nibbling a fresh basil leaf in July.

ACKNOWLEDGMENTS

Behind this book are invaluable friends who helped make its writing easier.

My wife, Joyce, offered encouragement, solace, and advice throughout the days and nights of writing and she protected me from the mental and physical wounds a commercial herb grower suffers during a turbulent and crazy spring. For over thirty years, she has given up much so I could play with words.

Dottie Jacobsen, my chief assistant in the greenhouse, has provided my horitcultural endeavors hawk-eyed protection for many years and I am grateful that her perceptive shield now extends to this literary effort. She also worked diligently and long with two other assistants, Rick Tagg and Laura Schneider, to give me extra time to cultivate words.

My special thanks to Art Tucker of Delaware State University for his willingness, over many years, to share his hard-won knowledge of herbs and for his patient translation of botanical information for a gardener who doesn't know a calyx from a corolla.

Although I'd like to take credit, the idea for this book came from Linda Ligon. Over the many years we've worked together, Linda has wielded her editor's pencil with creative skill and sensitivity; she is the kind of editor about whom writers dream.

This book would be just black and white without Joe Coca whose brilliance behind the lens created so many colorful photos that show more than words can say.

Lyle Craker and Jim Simon supplied helpful advice in person and through their invaluable publication, *The Herb, Spice, and Medicinal Plant Digest* (published by the University of Massachusetts cooperative extension system).

Gary Christensen knows how important he was in the process to get these words between covers; the advice was as good as the lunches.

A garden is an awful responsibility.

You never know what you may be aiding to grow in it.

—Charles Dudley Warner, 1874, *My Summer in a Garden*

CONTENTS

16

PLANTS
FROM SEED

20

PLANTS
FROM PLANTS

34

TRANSPLANTING
& THE FIRST YEAR

50

HERBS

Like a lot of herb gardeners, I'm often seized with the desire to plant just one more herb, to capture just one more heady aroma from a faraway place. One year, the passion was to possess yet another oregano (as if the more than two dozen types that are grown in the U.S.

. . . learning about herbs is both simple and complicated. The aroma of one sometimes mimics that of another, and several herbs may share the same common name.

weren't enough). I had heard about the quintessential oregano, a tiny-leaved Greek variety that was said to enliven food in a swirl of aroma.

For days, weeks, and months, this elusive plant was on my mind. Then one day a woman stopped in my greenhouse and chanced to recount the story of how her sister had brought just such an oregano to America from their little Greek village. (This was not a miraculous visitation; just another customer.) Greek women, she told me, not only used this oregano for its leaves, they lashed together dried stems to make basting brushes. She said it was a hardy plant: her sister grew this oregano in Minnesota where winters are frigid and white. And though its leaves were indeed tiny, she assured me that this oregano wasn't the variety of thyme (*Thymus pulegioides* 'Oregano-scented') which invariably disappoints taste buds that anticipate the real thing. She offered to have her sister bring some seeds to me next time she visited.

A few months after my conversation with this stranger, as Christmas neared, there was a knock on my door. There stood the woman and her sister; they thrust into my hands a plastic bag full of bare, brown stems topped with ripe seeds (I had to take their word that the leaves had been small). I put my nose inside the bag and inhaled the delightful fragrance of what I thought would be my long-sought oregano.

I had to know more about this oregano, so I called a botanist friend who has devoted most of his adult life to the study of herbs. He invited me to send him some of the branches and seeds.

A few days after I sent the sample, a short letter arrived from my friend. "Thanks for the summer savory seeds," he said. "Actually, this is not the first time that someone has sent me *Satureja hortensis* labeled as oregano. Don't feel too bad."

What a letdown. I always thought the Greeks invented oregano, and now I learn that they don't know the difference between an *Origanum* and a *Satureja*. Summer savory does indeed have small leaves, but it's an annual and temperatures much below freezing kill it. The reason it "came back" each year after a Minnesota deepfreeze is that it reseeds itself readily. The women in the little Greek village and their descendants in America aren't fools, but neither are they botanists. They let their nose and their sense of taste teach them what they need to know about herbs, and a misplaced name won't change that.

As my encounter with the small-leaved "Greek oregano" illustrates, learning about herbs is both simple and complicated. The aroma of one sometimes mimics that of another, and several herbs may share the same common name. Botanical names can offer more positive identification when they are properly applied, but there is nothing like personal experience with the plants themselves. In the end, it is your nose and your palate that must decide which herb offers the perfect aroma or flavor.

THE AROMA OF HERBS

The aroma of an herb, at once so simple and pure, is actually quite complex and mysterious. Under a microscope or magnifying glass, herb leaves and stems are wondrous landscapes filled with tiny hairs, craters, and mountains—and oil glands which contain the chemicals that produce the herb's particular scent. Minute ruptures in these oil sacs release the aroma when the foliage sways in a breeze or when a hand brushes its leaves.

Scientists aren't certain why plants produce the aromatic chemical soup that gives herbs their aroma and flavor. (Do they help in the reproductive process as attractants for pollinators, or are they life-preserving repellants?) For most of us, the "why" doesn't matter; we love the surprise of sniffing a sage that has a pineapple aroma; we stroke the tiny green leaves of a thyme and marvel that it smells of lemon; we glory in a bed of mint shimmering in the morning sun, giving off scents of oranges, lemons, apples, even lavenders; we bask in the heady, fruity fragrance of Sweet Annie and the spicy aroma of the curry plant. To the gardener, these herb fragrances are exciting and magical; to the scientist with expensive modern equipment, the chemicals that create the fragrances provide liquid fingerprints that can be used, along with traditional botanical methods, to precisely indentify plants. These essential oils are quite complex; one recent study of lavender iden-

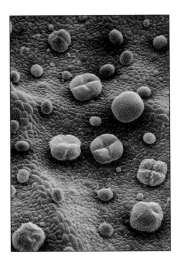

The four-celled head of the basil's oil gland can be seen in this 100X magnification.

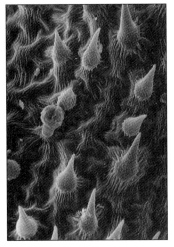

The upper side of a lemon balm leaf at 600X magnification.

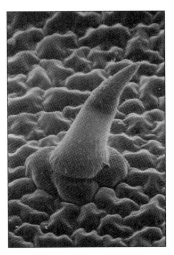

The upper surface of a peppermint leaf shows an oil gland in this 400X magnification.

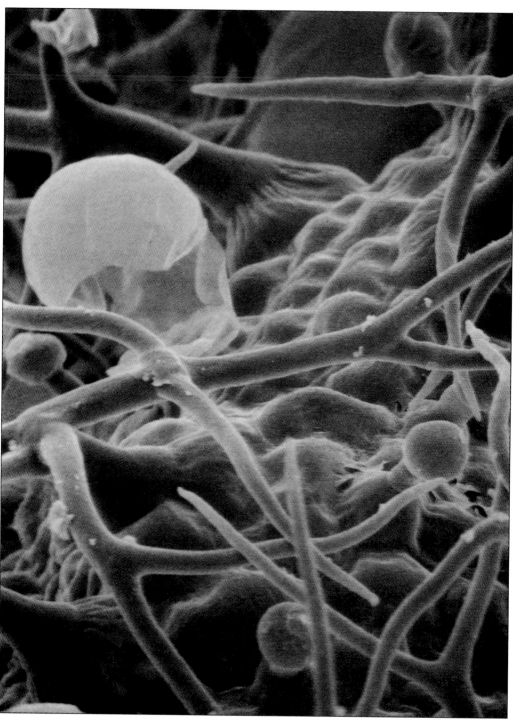

A lavender bud at 400X magnification looks like a tangle of tendrils. The prominent gland on the left has released so much of its essential oil that it has become a drop of oil with a wax cap.

tified more than thirty different chemicals in the fragrance-producing oil. The subtle variations in chemical makeup of similar plants mark important varietal differences and create changes in aroma. Other herbs have similar numbers of chemicals that work together to produce their fragrances.

To a European of the Mediterranean regions where herbs grow wild and in profusion, the idea of raising herbs in a garden is a bit cockeyed. But if you have only a few square feet of garden in which to seek solace from smog and congestion, as so many in this country do, the allure of all these glorious scents in a garden of one's own is strong.

HOW HERBS REPRODUCE

On those foreign hillsides where wild herbs grow, they reproduce themselves naturally. If you look at the ground carefully on one of those hillsides, you'll see seedlings sprouting and forcing their roots into the rocky soil at the same time they push their heads toward the sun; these plants come from seeds sown freely on the wind by the more mature perennial plants around them or by last year's crop of annuals. A short distance away, another population of plants slowly spreads as the branches that touch the ground sprout roots that dig into the soil and soon become self-sustaining. When branches do this, we call it layering. When the plants' underground roots or rhizomes branch off and send up new plants, we say the plants have spread by their roots. A little farther along our hillside there is a colony of plants that multiply from their bases; every year each plant has a larger base with more shoots coming from it; we say these herbs multiply from their crowns.

The different ways plants

Hearty starts of oregano, lovage, and variegated lemon thyme are ready for transplanting into the garden.

in a natural state increase their population, as well as other ways that require more human intervention, are easily put to use by the resourceful gardener. In the following pages we'll look at these methods in detail.

PLANTS FROM
SEED

Seeds are not dead, dry objects that spring to life; they are tender, living organisms at rest. Transforming these specks of dormant vitality into burgeoning plants is one of the great pleasures and challenges open to an herb gardener.

Even beyond the delightful qualities of form, color, symmetry, and possibility that can be seen and imagined in a seed, there is much that is hidden inside the seed coat until time and germination reveal it

One of the first things you notice about seeds is that even in their smallness there is beauty and complexity. The imperfect roundness of a tawny coriander fruit, etched with thin ribs that give it the illusion of toughness, is brittle and when cracked reveals two seeds, flat on one side and rounded on the other. A basil seed is a quick-change artist: at first it's a hard, black, oblong speck, but once wet, it turns gray-blue, soft, and gelatinous. You can sow thousands of seeds and still find small surprises, such as the day you realize for the first time that the tiny black seeds of onion chives are slightly smaller than those of garlic chives. Each herb's seed identifies it as surely as do its leaf form and fragrance. The exterior of an herb seed only hints at the world that lies inside it; the seed contains not only a miniature plant, but the idea of the garden.

Even beyond the delightful qualities of form, color, symmetry, and possibility that can be seen and imagined in a seed, there is much that is hidden inside the seed coat until time and germination reveal it. Germination takes place when a living seed absorbs enough water that the tiny organism can begin to use the energy of its stored food; too much or too little water, or soil temperatures too high or too low at this stage can cause the seed to die. Fortunately, the conditions needed for germination have fairly broad limits; otherwise there would be fewer plants and more frustrated gardeners in the world.

Not all seeds are perfect and alive, so not all of the ones in a packet will germinate. A few seed merchants print a germination rate on the packet, but most do not. This information can help you determine how many seeds to sow to produce the number of plants you want, but keep in mind that the seed has been tested under ideal conditions in a laboratory, and the conditions in your backyard garden may differ. Sometimes there is a reason for the absence of germination information. I called a big seed company one year to find the germination rate of the sweet woodruff seed it sold. The firm's chief horticulturist told me bluntly that it wasn't known because the company's staff didn't know how to germinate the seed. Seeds may germinate poorly for a variety of reasons. Harvest conditions may not have been ideal; seeds on most plants do not ripen simultaneously, and they are usually harvested when most seeds are ripe but before the first to ripen begin to scatter. Poor seed handling techniques after harvest may also contribute to low germination. The seeds of some herbs contain chemicals that inhibit germination until time or environmental conditions remove them; the chemicals sometimes prevent all the seeds from germinating at the same time or at the wrong time. This can be an advantage in nature, where a plant may produce seeds at a time of year when the success of seedlings would be poor.

A germination inhibitor is the reason that parsley takes so long to germinate. One way to break down the chemical is to place the seeds in old panty hose and soak them for a couple of days in an oxygenated aquarium. This soaking method speeds germination of parsley seed planted in cold ground but as the soil warms, germination improves without this step.

Soil temperature alone also affects the germination of many herb seeds: if it is too low, seeds rot before they sprout or they germinate poorly; if it is too high, tender embryos die or lie dormant until temperatures decrease. Most herb seeds germinate best when soil temperatures are between 55° and 75°F; the optimum is around 70°F.

Seeds of some herbs need to go through a real or simulated cold season before they will germinate. Unless they are left to self-sow outdoors, sweet cicely, echinacea, and angelica seeds should be refrigerated in a plastic bag of moist sphagnum peat moss until they are sown the following spring. Sweet cicely seeds will actually germinate in the refrigerator and should be transplanted to pots as soon as they do.

Some popular herbs just can't be grown from seed. French tarragon is virtually sterile; it seldom even flowers. Peppermint and Italian oregano (also called hardy marjoram) are hybrids and 99 percent sterile, according to Arthur O. Tucker, an herb taxonomist. In a landmark study of thyme plants, Harriet Flannery Phillips discovered that all English thyme plants have only female flowers, making it impossible to reproduce truly from seed; this condition may also account for the variability of other seed-grown thyme.

For all their complexities, seeds remain a prime means of starting herb plants because they can be stored for many months and even years, they are small and easy to ship, they are inexpensive, and little special equipment is needed to germinate and grow them into plants.

SOWING SEED OUTDOORS

Because most gardeners want only a few of each kind, herbs are not row crops in most gardens as are corn, beans, broccoli, lettuce, and other vegetables. If you want only two or three plants of a variety, whether annual, biennial, or perennial, it's not efficient to sow seed directly in an outside garden bed. If you want a dozen or more plants, though, direct sowing becomes more practical. The following popular annuals or biennials come easily from direct-sown seed: basil, borage, caraway, chamomile, chervil, coriander, dill, and parsley.

Some popular herbs just can't be grown from seed. French tarragon is virtually sterile; it seldom even flowers. Peppermint and Italian oregano (also called hardy marjoram) are hybrids and 99 percent sterile. . . .

Many perennial herbs that come true from seed are not usually direct-sown because their seeds might be tiny and difficult to handle, and the seedlings slow to grow after they've emerged. Perennial herbs with larger seeds or more rapid growth for direct seeding are angelica, anise hyssop, chives, lemon balm, lovage, sage, and sorrel.

PREPARING THE SEEDBED

Soil preparation is important to successful germination and growth of herb seeds. A good seedbed is level and rich in nutrients, deeply dug, quick draining, and composed of the finest earth without clods or

---

I put great faith in soil amendments; my favorites are good, crumbly composted vegetative matter and sphagnum peat that comes in compressed bales, usually from Canada.

---

stones. Unless you garden somewhere near the center of the universe (which is between Grundy Center and Eldora, Iowa), where Nature made the soil nearly perfect for growing anything, seedbed preparation may take some backbreaking work. Gardeners unlucky enough to live in areas of the United States that have sticky, heavy clay soil that dries brick hard or a sandy soil that refuses to hold moisture need to give their ground special attention—more than just turning the soil with a

fork and raking away the stones. Beds where seed will be sown need even better soil tilth than ordinary garden beds, but it is possible to create it even if your garden is located on an old abandoned driveway as is mine.

Unless your garden will be built on a concrete pad, it's probably not necessary to buy topsoil; I don't trust the stuff I've found in plastic bags with a topsoil label because the contents often doesn't look much different from the good old gold-colored Virginia clay with which I'm blessed. Instead, I put great faith in soil amendments; my favorites are good, crumbly composted vegetative matter (that's rotted leaves, grass clippings that have not been treated with herbicides, and vegetable kitchen scraps), and sphagnum peat that comes in compressed bales, usually from Canada. After I've turned the top foot of soil and removed stones, broken bottles, and other artifacts left by time and reduced all the clods to grainy smoothness with a garden fork, I thoroughly work into the soil about 6 inches of damp compost or peat moss; the result is soft, smooth and porous. When I use this much peat moss (or composted hardwood leaves), I dust garden lime over the entire bed until it looks as if there had been a light snow; the lime will counteract the acidity of the peat or the leaves and my naturally acidic soil, resulting in a soil

pH of about 6 to 6.5—perfect for most herbs. To verify that your soil is properly balanced and neither too acid (low pH) or too sweet (high pH), call your local U.S. Agriculture Extension Service office for information on how to have your soil tested.

If you're a fan of manure and live where it is readily available, help yourself to some of the dried, composted stuff and spread a couple of inches of it over the new garden bed and thoroughly mix it into the top foot; manure is low in nutrients and gives up what it does have slowly, but it is a fine soil conditioner. Finally, add an all-purpose fertilizer, either organic or inorganic; a slow release fertilizer such as Osmocote 14-14-14* lasts through a normal gardening season.

Fertilizers formulated for soilless growing media used for containers often add trace elements, minute quantities of minerals found in normal soils that plants need also.

If you can straighten up after all this digging and soil preparation, stand back and admire your newly raised garden bed. It's wise to put stones or wood around the edges to keep the new garden soil from washing away during hard rains.

---

*The numbers on a fertilizer bag disclose the percentages of nitrogen (N), phosphorous (P), and water soluble potassium (K) in the formula; they are the essential nutrients for plant growth. The remainder of the contents of the bag is a neutral material called a carrier.

Sowing seed is as low-tech as it was 2000 years ago; all you need is a stick or a finger to scratch a row and some labels to mark the rows and identify the seedlings when they germinate. Most herb seed germinates quite well when scattered in rows and covered with 1/4 inch of soil; spacing is not critical at this point, although seeds needn't be too close together.

The seed of some herbs needs light to germinate, but this fact is easily misconstrued; it doesn't mean seeds need a tan before they will germinate. The large seed of borage will get enough light if planted a half-inch deep in loose soil, according to Lyle Craker of the University of Massachusetts, one of the top soil scientists in the U.S. who knows herbs; smaller seeds would need to be closer to the surface. Other seeds needing light are angelica, dill, echinacea, feverfew, and wormwood.

Covering the seed *is* important, however, because it brings the seed in contact with the dampened soil whose moisture wakes it up to grow; but seed covered too deeply may lack enough energy to send its sprout all the way up into the sunshine. The rule of thumb for most seeds is to sow them to a depth twice the seed diameter. Seedbed soil should remain damp but not soggy until seedlings emerge; for seedlings that take several weeks, such as parsley, gardeners sometimes place a board or other cover over the row to lessen water evaporation and keep weeds down until seeds germinate. Competition for food and light from weeds is often a big problem for seedlings struggling into the world, and the prudent gardener will keep a weed-free seedbed.

After seedlings emerge, don't let them wilt from lack of water, but also do not water them too often; root-rot and fungus diseases get a quick start when soil is kept too wet. Plant roots need air and the water, while necessary for plant growth, fills the air pockets in the soil and can suffocate roots. It's best to water in the morning so that seedlings don't spend the night drowning; during the day water evaporates from the soil quickly. Apply an all-purpose water-soluble fertilizer fortnightly for six weeks after germination to speed early growth.

TRANSPLANTING OUTDOOR-GROWN SEEDLINGS

If you plan to grow seedlings to maturity where you sowed them in an outdoor garden, thin them to the spacing suggested in the chart on pages 56–61; this thinning will permit the plants to grow without close competition for air, light, water, and nutrients. I never bother to thin dill and coriander seedlings because the plants mature so quickly and I am interested in the early foliage growth rather than the mature growth which produces seeds; I just scissor off enough foliage to use in the kitchen. The foliage will regrow on these seedlings and as many as five crops can be harvested.

Sowing seed where plants will grow eliminates the transplant step that slows growth and increases risks, but sometimes transplanting is necessary, especially if you have established a nursery area, cold frame, or special seedbed in

---

Among those seeds needing light [to germinate] are angelica, borage, dill, echinacea, feverfew, and wormwood.

---

your garden. Cloudy, damp spring days are made for transplanting seedlings from the seedbed to the main garden. Dig the seedlings with as little damage as possible to the roots; I transplant outdoor-grown seedlings in little groups of four or five to lessen shock caused by torn roots. This method, which I call "clump transplanting", is explained in detail on pages 30–32.

When I was a child, one of the jobs I enjoyed most in the garden was finding twigs to stick through 6-inch squares of paper to make little umbrellas which I placed carefully over the seedlings my father had transplanted and watered. The twig-and-paper umbrellas lessened the shock of transplanting by tempering the sun's dehydrating effects. Now we have wonderful new materials like spun-bonded, polyester row covers that do this and more. This translucent fabric permits light, air, and water to pass through while it shields young seedlings from hot sun, cold winds, torrential rains, and an assortment of insects; it also gives some protection against squirrels and birds, which are sometimes spring predators of seedlings.

For all the changes and new equipment, the basics of seed starting remain unaltered from when I was a boy or when Pliny the Elder gardened in the first century A.D.

After seeds germinate, the gardener becomes aware quickly of the vulnerability of tender, young seedlings. One summer not long ago, I sowed several 3-foot rows with dill, coriander, and basil seeds; I intended to use this test plot for a photo essay on the life of a seedling. Late one afternoon a few days later, I checked and saw that the seedlings had emerged. I decided to take some photos the following morning of the two rows of purple basil. Bright and early, with camera at the ready, I discovered that a troop of slugs had munched the basil into history overnight. The incident produced a shorter photo essay than I had intended, but it reminded me in no uncertain terms of the hazards of leaving unprotected young seedlings in the hands of Mother Nature. (Methods of controlling slugs are discussed on page 53.)

STARTING SEED INDOORS

I started gardening in the days before small, cheap plastic pots, and in those days most gardens were started by planting seeds directly in the soil. If you purchased seedlings, you got them at a nursery where a man with rough-hewn hands scooped them up from a wooden flat, wrapped the tender young, green shoots in a piece of yesterday's newspaper, and handed them to you; failure often attended attempts to transplant these bare-root seedlings. Times have changed: it is easy to purchase little potted plants to place in the garden, and wonderful success almost always follows. But a range of simple and inexpensive techniques are available to home gardeners who wish to start their own seedlings indoors for transplant to a backyard garden. Today there is no reason why a home gardener can't produce a potted herb as good as or better than one for sale at a nursery. The advantages of growing your own are many: you'll have the variety you want when you want it, you won't have to wait on the weather to get started (as the outdoor gardener will), and an early start will provide you with a plant that is larger earlier and will produce more. You can start tiny, slow-growing perennial seeds (such as 98,200-seeds-per-ounce thyme or 165,000-seeds-per-ounce sweet marjoram), or slow-to-start parsley easily and early enough to give you a jump of several months over plants propagated outdoors.

For all the changes and new equipment, the basics of seed starting remain unaltered from when I was a boy or when Pliny the Elder gardened in the first century A.D. Gardening is a balancing act, and it is no more evident than when a gardener decides to start seedlings indoors for transplanting. The key is to create an artificial environment that duplicates the most perfect conditions a seed might encounter outdoors: the light has to be steady and days should be long; water should appear just when needed and in only the right amount; temperatures should be ideal for germination and growth; a steady supply of nutrients to provide uninterrupted growth should be available; and the air should move through the

Fluorescent tubes are positioned no more than 4 inches above new seedlings.

Shelves in a basement room, each equipped with a bank of lights, create space for thousands of seedlings.

Chicken-wire doors on the light benches keep out the author's wayward cats.

seedlings and caress their tender, new growth to keep them dry. To achieve and manage such environmental control is a large responsibility and it takes some skill, knowledge, and maybe a bit of artistry; the basics can be learned quickly, but a technique will become perfected through use, observation, and failure. The indoor gardener needs to know much more than an outdoor counterpart who gambles that Nature will take care of almost everything.

My seed-starting experience began on a windowsill, and I learned quickly that the wan, late winter light that reached inside lacked the predictability, intensity, and day length to keep plants stocky; my plants were as leggy as a shoestring and as easily broken as a piece of dried capellini. I knew there must be a bet-

ter way, and there was.

Little space is needed indoors to start seedlings. Fluorescent lights are the most important element in the indoor garden. Two 4-foot-long double-tube fluorescent fixtures placed side by side create about the right light intensity to produce sixty-four plants in $2^{1}/_{2}$-inch pots. (That's an area 1 foot wide by 40 inches long.) These fixtures can be hung by chains over a table so they can be raised and lowered as necessary. Special plant lights are not necessary; I have used cool white fluorescent tubes for years with excellent results. To keep the seedlings from stretching, position the tubes no more than 4 inches from the tops of the seedlings; as they grow and are transplanted from flats into pots, the lights will have to be adjusted. My own little grow-

ing area, in my low-ceilinged, unheated basement, receives no natural light. To further conserve growing space, I've installed lights in a bunk-bed arrangement that has four levels (each one is 2 feet by 8 feet) and is about 6 feet high; in that space I can produce enough seedlings for my herb business to fill 12,000 pots every two weeks. A timer set for 16 hours on, eight hours off, relieves me from having to be around to turn my light garden off and on.

THE GROWING MEDIUM

The idea of a growing medium without soil may seem contrary to nature, but for many years I have used soilless growing mixes for seed starting and for growing seedlings. I have been quite happy with them because they are disease and weed free, store

Soilless medium should be damp and scooped loosely into pots or seed flats. Packing prevents good aeration.

easily, hold moisture yet drain well, and give consistent results. Soilless media are made from natural substances such as sphagnum peat moss, composted peanut hulls, composted bark, perlite, and vermiculite.

I wet soilless mixes just before filling germination containers, adding enough water to dampen the mix but keep it loose at the same time; storing the mix wet invites disease organisms to take up residence. Almost any shallow, clean, disease-free container with drainage holes can be used to germinate seeds. In my work, I use virgin plastic flats that are 11 inches by 21 inches and are 2½ inches deep. Smaller containers such as pots work equally well for a small number of seedlings. Used pots can be sterilized

with a solution of a half cup of chlorine bleach to a gallon of water, with enough detergent added to scrub away any accumulated dirt and mineral deposits. The container should not be over 2½ inches deep and should not be filled all the way to the top. (Deeper plastic pots should be cut down.) If the sides of the container stand too far above the growing medium, air cannot circulate well through the seedlings, and disease may become a problem. The volume of growing medium is important because it affects the water-holding capacity of the seedling container. I've found that 1½ to 2 inches of growing medium in the container is about the right amount to allow good moisture control, and also give the seedling roots ample room.

The simplest way to start seedlings is to sow a single variety of seed directly in a pot and grow it there until it's ready to go into the garden. Almost any herb can be direct-sown, but I've found that nasturtiums and chives work well with this method because they naturally grow in clumps and lack the traditional plant stem. The quality of herb seedlings is enhanced by transplanting because, as you'll see later, it allows the grower an opportunity to control seedling stem elongation; this is a condition that leads to poor-quality, wispy plants that twine snake-like over the pot's edge.

SOWING SEED INDOORS

I sow most herb seed in rows rather than scattering it over the surface of the growing medium; air circulation through seedlings grown in rows is better, an important factor in eliminating disease problems. I use a small strip of metal that is V-shaped in cross-section to press furrows into the dampened growing medium; I then scatter the seeds into the depressions.

It probably doesn't matter whether the seeds are covered with growing medium after they are sown; the moisture content in the flats remains high enough that the seeds drink it up without being covered. If the seeds are left uncovered, you can actually watch them swell and see the first roots emerge. (The chart on pages 62–65 lists my preferences for covering seed; because it takes longer for germination to show when seeds are covered, the number of days to germination may vary when my suggestions for covering are not followed.)

How much seed to sow and how thickly to sow it are questions that I must face annually. The amount of seed to sow depends on how many plants you want of a given variety and the germination rate of that variety. The seeding technique also plays a critical role. I have agonized over the placement of single seeds, struggling with the tiny specks to make sure they were separated in the rows by half an

A strip of angled metal stock makes neat furrows for seeding.

Coriander seed is sown thickly into the furrows.

Covering the seeds loosely with growing medium is optional in most cases; I prefer to cover coriander.

Large seeds such as those of nasturtium can be handled differently than the smaller varieties.

Seeds are dibbled into individual pots, two per pot, at a depth three to four times the diameter of the seed.

Additional soilless mix is sprinkled over the seed depressions and patted lightly into place. These seeds should germinate in ten days and be ready to transplant (with two or more true leaves) in five or six more days.

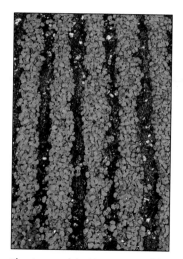

Planting seed thickly isn't wasteful; it makes for hearty, stocky clumps when the seedlings are transplanted.

An even, gentle spray settles the growing medium and starts the germination process.

Plastic wrap or clear plastic lids hold moisture until seeds begin to germinate.

inch or so. Although this may be necessary when sowing seed for which you paid ten or fifteen cents apiece (as with hybrid geranium seeds), most herb seed isn't that costly and my transplanting technique doesn't work nearly as well when seeds are spaced so far apart. So make it easy and don't worry about spacing invidual seeds; they can touch, and in some cases it's best to sow them so thickly that they are piled on top of each other (as with parsley and other traditionally low germination, or difficult-to-germinate herbs).

Many experienced gardeners would shudder at how thickly I sow seeds, because thick stands of seedlings sometimes invite disease problems, especially when the seedling flats are in a greenhouse, where environmental conditions cannot be controlled as

precisely as under lights. On the other hand, sowing thickly is quick and makes transplanting much easier, as you'll see. Be sure to label each row of seedlings, or mark pots with a water-proof maker so you will know what's in them.

After the seed is sown, water the pots or flats with a gentle, even spray so that water is evenly distributed (I use the spray at my kitchen sink). To keep the water from evaporating while waiting for the seed to germinate, I tape plastic wrap over the pots or flats. Pots or flats may also be slipped into clear plastic bags; clear plastic domes are available for flats. If you are starting seed in winter or early spring, choose a room in the house that is bright and has warm, even heat between 70° and 80°F; place the flats or pots so that direct sunshine

will not hit them. I sometimes find it necessary to place a piece of cardboard over my flats; even winter sun can melt a plastic dome or cook seed to death. When I sow seeds in summer to produce fall plants, I place the flats in an airconditioned room because daytime temperatures otherwise might prove too high for good germination. I often stack flats that are covered with humidity domes three or four high to conserve space; this does not affect germination.

Now the vigil begins; I check at least twice a day to watch for the first signs of seedling emergence. As soon as I notice the most minute evidence of germination (even if it's only a few scattered seedlings), I remove the plastic wrap or the humidity domes and place the containers under fluorescent lights;

the lights produce enough heat to maintain 70° to 75°F daytime temperatures, but night temperatures when the lights are off may drop into the sixties. It's usually not necessary to water the seedlings when they first go under the lights because the plastic covering has maintained moisture levels during germination. The temperature under the lights and the moisture level in the seedling container will determine how quickly a flat or pot of seedlings dries; it is often not necessary to water the seedlings until the second or third day after germination. It's easy to see when the seedlings need water because the peat moss in the soilless mix lightens in color as it becomes dry.

Moisture is the key to seedling growth, but too much water can lead to a quick death; how and when the seedlings are watered is critical to their survival. Although many growers use chemical drenches to control seedling diseases, I think diseases can be controlled as well by manipulating the seedling environment. I water my seedlings each morning soon after the lights come on and then let them dry during the day and through the night. This routine reduces problems with foliage diseases spread by water and checks root rot and other similar diseases. Under lights, there is steady warmth and light, and I can count on the growing medium to dry

out predictably, which makes it easier to judge when and how much to water. Watering close to the dark period, inside or outside, soaks seedling roots at a time that it is difficult for the plant to lose the moisture; this means the roots have a longer period of time during which the air pockets around them are filled with water and this can become a problem. A fan set on low speed to push air through the seedlings will help seedling foliage dry after watering and prevent the buildup of heat produced by the lights. The fan also helps to dry the growing medium with air movement over its surface.

I'm so low-tech that I still use a little plastic watering can with a tapering spout that I've had for years. I direct the flow of water between the rows to keep from knocking down the seedlings; by adjusting the angle of the watering can, I can easily control the flow of water to prevent growing medium from washing over them. If the surface of the growing medium does not look dry the next morning, I know that I am applying too much water, so I cut back that morning, or don't water at all. Seedlings can withstand more dryness than many gardeners believe.

When you water, make sure all the growing medium is wet; water running out the bottom of a pot or flat is one indication. However, growing medium with a high peat con-

A pale, dry surface signals that it's time to water; a carefully directed fine stream won't knock down tiny seedlings.

tent is sometimes difficult to wet if it has become too dry, and water applied from the top can run through without penetrating to the roots. You may need to water a second or third time to thoroughly wet the medium; this is especially true of pots in which the growing medium has pulled away from the pot walls as it has dried, allowing the water to run down the sides and out the bottom. Keen observation is important during watering because you've got to get it right; overwatering is the leading cause of plant and seedling mortality.

FEEDING SEEDLINGS

A liquid fertilizer applied during watering will produce amazing results in seedling quality that will follow it into the garden. Most commer-

The first true leaves of these coriander seedlings are barely visible on some plants; spent seed cases still cling to the tips of some seed leaves.

A flat of purple basil seedlings with first true leaves just beginning to show. Note the occasional green "rogue"; purple basils often don't come true from seed.

cially available growing media have enough fertilizer to feed plants and seedlings for a week or two; I begin my regular feeding schedule after the seedlings have been under lights for a week. I recommend use of an organic or inorganic water-soluble fertilizer, at the manufacturer's recommended strength, applied at least once a week when you water. (Fish emulsion or Peters 20-10-20 work well, but any plant food can be used.) The importance of feeding even little seedlings was underscored by research conducted in Israel by Eli Putievsky. Fertilizing herbs such as marjoram, lemon balm, and thyme at each watering with a nutrient solution half the recommended strength resulted in plants that were double and triple the size of unfertilized ones after sixty days; that's a tremendous head start for plants to have as they go into the garden.

TRANSPLANTING INDOOR-GROWN SEEDLINGS

The first leaves that appear on a seedling differ in shape from the plant's later leaves and are called the cotyledons, seed leaves, or nurse leaves. The next leaves that emerge are the true leaves, and as soon as seedlings produce a set of these true leaves, it is time to transplant them. If left untransplanted, the seedlings will become stringy and too crowded for proper growth and they will be impossible to untangle for transplanting.

When transplanting seedlings into pots from the flats in which they germinated, you'll need to be very careful of their roots. Because new seedlings' root systems are minimal, very little growing medium will cling to them when you move the plants. Transplanting bare-rooted seedlings can cause considerable stress to young plants and must be done with care.

This problem aside, I have yet to find a seedling grown under lights indoors that can't be transplanted; this includes parsley, coriander, dill, and all the others about which warnings are traditionally offered. The gardener's control of the environment indoors or in a greenhouse is the reason that it is so easy to transplant these herbs successfully.

I use plastic pots that are 2 to 2½ inches square at the top and fill them with the same soilless growing medium I used to start the seedlings, dampening it before use in the same way. Pots should be sterile to avoid disease problems; plastic pots are easier to sterilize with chlorine bleach and soap (as described on page 26) than those made from clay or foam.

I've developed a special technique for transplanting seedlings into pots for later planting in the garden that I believe lessens stress on the seedlings and creates healthier plants more quickly than traditional procedures; plants grown this way are more like-

To begin clump transplanting, gently break out a row of thickly planted seedlings.

Break the row into smaller clumps, keeping as much growing medium around the roots as possible.

Gently massage the root clumps so they can be broken easily into small groups of three to five or six plants.

It's important to work quickly so that delicate roots won't dry out.

Holding a clump by its leaves, dibble a hole in each pot with an index finger or other blunt instrument.

Be sure not to pack the growing medium as you set the clumps in place.

ly to have larger harvests, as well. I call my method clump transplanting. Instead of removing single seedlings and dibbling them into pots, I gently break a row of seedlings into small clumps of up to five seedlings. I don't count them, but take what comes apart most easily with the least root

I settle the clump into the hole gently, but deeper than it was growing in the seedling flat. The depth to which the clump is set depends on where the nurse leaves, not the true leaves, are located on the stem. I try to place the clump deep enough that the true leaves are level with the growing medium and the nurse leaves are covered.

damage. It would defeat the beneficial effects of this method to prick out individual seedlings and gather them in clumps. The size of the clump usually depends on the physical stature of the seedlings; the larger the leaves, the fewer seedlings in the clump. I aim to create the immediate appearance of a branched plant without having to wait many weeks for it to happen naturally through numerous prunings of the tiny stems. The clump starts out with a larger root mass in the pot than a single seedling would have, which helps to take up water faster than would an individual seedling; in a small way, this accelerates the drying of the growing medium and lessens the problems of root and stem rot.

The actual transplanting is also a bit different from traditional methods. I hold the clump of seedlings by their leaves so as not to damage the soft stems (damaged stems offer an entry to disease organisms that cause stem rot). While I hold the clump in one hand, I shove the index finger of my free hand into the center of the pot into which the clump will go. I settle the clump into the hole gently, but *deeper than it was growing in the seedling flat*. The depth to which the clump is set depends on where the nurse leaves, not the true leaves, are located on the stem. I try to place the clump deep enough that the true leaves are level with the growing medium and the nurse leaves are covered. This depth isn't always possible, but the seedlings should stand upright in the center of the pot even after watering. I

A gentle watering will settle the growing medium around the clumps' roots without packing it.

This coriander seedling was transplanted from flat to pot two weeks ago, and is ready for the garden.

water the seedling clumps lightly right after transplanting to settle the growing medium around the roots.

After transplanting, I put the pots back under fluorescent lights, raising the lights if necessary to accommodate the height of the pot but still keeping the lights only a few inches from the top of the plant. I continue to water and fertilize the potted seedlings as they begin to fill out; the transplants should be ready for the garden in three to six weeks. I judge a seedling ready for the garden when its foliage has spread to the edge of the pot and when there is sufficient root growth to hold the growing medium together when the plant is gently knocked out of the pot for inspection.

HARDENING OFF

The one drawback to growing plants indoors under lights is that stems and leaves are soft and the plants cannot be placed in the garden as soon as they are ready; it is necessary to acclimate them to the vicissitudes of the outdoor environment. Gardeners call this process "hardening off", a term that describes the stiffening of the tender tissues of the stem and leaves.

Cold frames, basically bottomless boxes with clear lids that can be raised for ventilation, are the traditional way to protect plants while introducing them to the real world of wide temperature swings, strong sunlight, and stiff breezes. If you don't have a cold frame, you can put young potted plants in a place that receives morning sun only and is protected from wind, bringing the plants in each night; follow this procedure for three days. For the next three days, give the potted plants a more open location and leave them out at night as long as it is above freezing. This will prepare them for planting on the seventh day.

A less complicated way to harden off transplants is to place the pots in the garden and cover them with a thin layer of spun-bonded row cover. (If the weather changes to brutal cold it's easier to bring the seedlings in if they're in pots.) Row cover not only protects tender foliage from burning but allows water to trickle through it, and at night provides some protection from cold. After four or five days under a row cover, the potted plants are ready to be transplanted. For the appropriate times to transplant specific herbs, see the chart on pages 62–65.

Now that your herbs are at home in the garden, you can sit back and enjoy them with the knowledge that you have worked with nature to nurture a small speck of life into something much larger and more wonderful. At the same time, you have the opportunity to watch a little part of the world with which you have an intimate relationship live in its time. You've earned that sense of pride that comes with self-sufficiency.

PLANTS FROM
PLANTS

The reproductive power of seeds is complex and mysterious, but when a bit of branch from an herb sprouts roots and becomes a plant on its own, we call it a rooted cutting and think it happens almost like magic. Herbs, and many other plants, are capable of even more asexual sorcery. To make new plants, roots (and rhizomes) can be divided, plant crowns can be separated into new plants, and branches that touch the ground can form roots and the rooted portion can become independent from the parent plant.

There is really no magic that animates the asexual reproduction of plants; it's all a matter of genes. All the genetic information about a plant is contained in each of its cells, and under the right conditions, it's possible for a segment of a plant to reproduce its missing parts and make a new plant that is genetically identical to its parent. It would be magical indeed if plants could do this whenever they wished, but they can't; certain environ-

mental factors, including human intervention, must be present for it to happen.

Vegetative propagation is the only way in which many important culinary, medicinal, and fragrant herbs can be

Herbs with variegated foliage generally can't be propagated by seed. Cuttings or divisions are the best guarantee that the offspring will resemble the parent, as in this *Lavandula dentata* 'Linda Ligon'.

propagated. Perennial herbs such as artemisia, thyme, santolina, rosemary, mint, lavender, sage, and oregano have many cultivated varieties that

are not reliably true to type when grown from seed; as a general rule, it's prudent to propagate all named cultivars vegetatively. Other herbs produced vegetatively are those that are sterile or those for which seed is not readily available. You'll find vegetative propagation convenient and fast if you want a few new plants from a friend's garden or a space-saving way to overwinter tender herbs indoors, or if it's time to replace a favorite sage, savory, or lavender that is becoming woody and unproductive.

LAYERING STEMS

Creating new plants by layering stems is ridiculously simple; many perennial herbs (chamomile, santolina, southernwood, winter savory, creeping and English thymes, prostrate rosemary, lavender, Vietnamese coriander, and a number of others) do it without prompting. A stem touches the moist ground, and before you know it that stem has put down roots. When plants per-

—continued on page 36

VARIETAL SELECTION

Besides choosing stems that are vigorous and healthy, varietal appearance is also important, especially in variegated herbs, many of which have occasional stems that are atypical. Golden lemon thyme, for instance, often has poor variegation on some stems and may even have stems with solid green leaves; these atypical stems will remain green if you root them. On the other hand, an extraordinarily beautiful or unusually variegated stem can be propagated by rooting. In fact, this is how many new cultivars are made available to the public.

Years ago I ordered some cuttings of Rober's Lemon Rose scented geranium; in the first shipment, I received rooted cuttings that were typical but in the next shipment, they all resembled another scented geranium, Old Fashioned Rose. I asked the propagator to explain the mix-up and was told that he had two "forms" of Rober's Lemon Rose, one with a "cut leaf" and one with a "potato leaf". What he had, of course, were two separate scented geranium varieties, even though they had both come from the same parent. Just because a plant has a name doesn't mean that a stem which shows a genetic change should carry the same name. (It can be a new variety, or it can look like its pre-hybridization parent.)

Sometimes genetic changes, when they

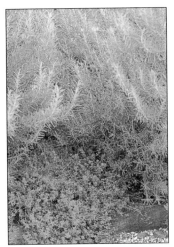

Golden Rain rosemary (*Rosmarinus officinalis* 'Joyce DeBaggio')

represent a new variety, are worth propagating; a single stem on an otherwise all dark green rosemary plant sported golden margins and green centers and became my Golden Rain rosemary (*Rosmarinus officinalis* 'Joyce DeBaggio'). Had I not been able to root this single stem tip, this highly decorative and aromatic evergreen shrub would not have come to be. Hybridizing seeds may be the classic method for obtaining new varieties, but genetic variations, or sports, are sometimes just as important. And any gardener may be lucky enough to discover sports like this one.

This thyme grew from a natural layering when a branch from the parent plant came in contact with the soil and rooted.

To move it to a new location, lift the plant gently to keep as much soil as possible around its roots.

Sharp shears divide one layered plant into several, each with a healthy root system.

form this multiplying feat without your assistance, count your blessings, check to see that new roots are well established, sever the connection between mother plant and off-spring with a sharp knife or scissors, gently dig the new plant, and place it in a new home.

Upright, woody-stemmed herbs with flexible branches can also be layered with your assistance. You won't need fancy equipment to prevent wilting as you might with rooting cuttings; after you've set some layers, you can forget about them until it's time to move the new plants or present them as potted gifts to friends.

Gardeners soon discover the axiom that it's easy for plants to do things on their own, but as soon as a gardener steps in to urge the plant to

do it, difficulties begin. This is true even of something as simple as layering. To make layering work better for you, it will help to know what factors induce plant stems to root: absence of light at the point where roots are to develop, constant soil moisture, good aeration, and moderate temperatures. It's not difficult to achieve these conditions outdoors. Soil, the key ingredient, provides the darkness and holds the moisture. If it's a good loose soil, aeration will take care of itself. For optimum temperatures, begin layering when temperatures moderate in late winter or spring.

Select a stem near the ground that is young and flexible. Beginning at a point 3 to 4 inches from the tip, strip about 5 inches of foliage from the stem. After removing the leaves and saving them to use

in the kitchen, use a sharp knife to scrape the thin bark off 2 or 3 inches of the underside of the leafless stem; this step, called wounding, seems to accelerate rooting in some species. Dig a small hole 2 to 3 inches deep with gently sloping sides below the prepared stem, and carefully lay it in the hole. Occasionally, it is necessary to peg it with a U-shaped wire or hairpin so it won't move, and cover it with soil. (If the soil in your garden is stiff or very sandy, fill the hole with a mixture of equal parts of sphagnum peat moss and perlite.) Mulch the area to keep the layering site moist or water it judiciously without soaking the plant roots and foliage; overwatering may invite disease.

Layered stems may form roots in several weeks or months, depending on the size of the stem and the herb chosen; layering is not a technique for the impatient. When a gentle tug on the stem meets with resistance, the stem is probably rooted and a careful visual inspection is called for. When it is ready, snip the rooted stem free and lift it gently to retain as much soil as possible around its roots. Then pot the plant or set it directly into a new location in the garden (see Transplanting Rooted Cuttings, page 49).

Commercial herb growers rarely propagate herbs by layering because a single plant can produce only a few progeny at once this way, but it is an excellent technique for most home gardeners because it is easy, requires no equipment at all, and almost always works.

DIVISIONS

While many herbs creep around, sending out roots from their stems on top of the soil, others secretly spread underground from crowns, roots, offsets, and specialized stems such as stolons and rhizomes. Mint stolons are the street gangs of the garden and take new territory with eager stealth. At first glance, the stolons look like roots themselves, but if you look carefully you'll see hairy roots dangling from them. Tarragon rhizomes are fleshy, and in spring, as vernal forces wake the plant, tiny buds swell on the rhizomes and burst into new stems;

these are the children in need of separation from their parent. Sorrel greets the first warmth of the late winter with clusters of new sprouts from its firm ocher crown. Proper and prim, *Origanum × majoricum* (often sold as hardy marjoram or Italian oregano) grows from a tangled mound of stems, which is easily severed into clumps that will make new plants. The many offsets of tough, slender chives are quickly divided by strong fingers into many little clumps. (A single chive bulblet looks silly all alone, but will multiply eventually.) Sweet woodruff, lemongrass, bee balm, Silver King artemisia, and catnip are other herbs that are easy to multiply by division.

When the tiny, green-capped stems of French tarragon push their heads through the early spring soil, my heart leaps with joy; it is time to make new plants by dividing vigorous old ones. It is probably the oldest method for multiplying herbs, and certainly the easiest and quickest way. Spring's cool, damp weather is the ideal time for the job, but plants can also be divided in the fall if similar climatic conditions prevail. A spade and sharp knife are the only tools you'll need for this rough surgery; the limited number of genetically identical offspring that you'll produce with them will be ready for harvesting almost immediately. Dividing herbs regularly has other benefits: it dis-

Some Herbs That Divide Easily

Mints

Tarragon

Sorrel

Italian oregano

Chives

Sweet woodruff

Lemongrass

Bee balm

Catnip

Silver King artemisia

Lemon balm

To divide a crown of French sorrel, carefully dig up as much root as possible.

Cut into the crown vertically with a sharp knife.

Leave each part with as much root as possible.

courages disease by thinning foliage and it controls rambunctious spreading.

The best candidates for division are herbaceous perennials, herbs, or other plants that die back each winter and pop up in the spring larger than they were the year before. Ignore the thin struggling plants with little vigor and less yen for life; choose instead vigorous specimens with many young stems pushing their way into the spring sun.

There are two ways to go about this division business, and in all probability the method you choose gives clues to your character. If you're the kind of gardener who plans ahead (don't we all wish we did), you'll mark the plants you want to divide in the fall before their tops die back to the ground; they'll be easier to find come spring. If you're the

other kind of gardener, you'll have to remember where the plants that you want to divide are located and you'll need to

The crown of a sorrel plant may produce only two or three new plants, but a vigorous tarragon or mint plant may have the potential for dozens.

be able to recognize them by their junior tufts that appear early. If you're in a hurry, you can bluster right in and carve up a clump on the soil surface with a shovel, imagining the location of its roots from the

location of its young shoots; this method may be inexact and yield few plants, but it is quick and clean, and the divisions usually wind up with lots of roots for an unhindered new start.

If you've got plenty of time and want the maximum number of plants, dig gingerly around the circumference of the plant, and pry the clump carefully from the ground. Lay the mass of roots out in the shade and massage the dirt away (or wash it off with a hose). The buds that show at the top of the root clumps are guides to where to perform surgery. With a sharp knife, divide the mass of roots, stolons, or rhizomes into fragments that have several new buds each. I try to obtain as large a root system as I can with each division. The crown of a sorrel plant may produce only two or three new plants, but a vigorous tarragon or mint plant may have the potential for dozens.

If the weather is hot when the urge to divide your herbs comes upon you, I suggest transplanting the divisions into pots and placing them in a shaded cold frame or other protected spot until the new root systems are well established. This procedure is useful also whenever your divisions have only one or two roots each. The larger the divisions, the less the transplant shock; carving up a plant with a knife or shovel can prove stressful even to a rampaging mint.

One caveat should be mentioned about divisions. Because they carry roots and garden soil with them, they can spread diseases and root insects such as nematodes from infected soils. This might be a major concern for a commercial grower with a large investment but should pose little or no anxiety for the home gardener.

ROOTING STEM CUTTINGS

I first watched a "stick" sprout roots and turn into a plant when I was a child and my mother cut the tip off an angel-wing begonia stem and put it in a glass of water on the kitchen windowsill. In a short time, it put forth a tangle of roots. Mom transplanted it to a pot, and it became a household ornament. Many years passed before I had a glimmer of the biological force that wheedles roots from a piece of stem. Now, after observing hundreds of thousands of cuttings root, I retain a reverence and wonder for this life-creating process.

ROOTING CUTTINGS IN WATER

Mom's method of rooting begonias works quite well for many herbs, and it's virtually trouble-free. All you need are some water, a windowsill, and a small glass, jar, or styrofoam cup. I spent a recent summer experimenting with rooting herb cuttings in water and I can tell you that this method, in some instances, will root cuttings as fast for you as my expensive automated propagation gadgets can for me. This method almost totally eliminates plant stress, which can slow rooting, and it avoids some of the wilts and rots that plague home gardeners when they try to root cuttings in other ways.

WHAT WORKS

Plant Propagation: Principles and Practices, by Hudson T. Hartmann and Dale E. Kester, a text used by students and many professional propagators, gives Mom's method a vote of confidence; it states that water is a suitable medium for rooting cuttings of easily propagated species. I've found that many herbs fit that category. Most of the herbs I tried rooted within two weeks or less: mints (a couple of varieties) in seven days, five vari-

Some Herbs That Root Easily in Water

Mint

Basil

Pineapple sage

Lemon verbena

Rosemary

Scented geraniums

Lavender

eties of basil in five to ten days, patchouli in ten, pineapple sage in eleven, and lemon verbena and a cultivar of rosemary in fourteen days. (Although basil is usually grown from seed, some new cultivars, such as Silver Fox, Aussie Sweetie, Mulberry Dance, and Holly's Painted, to name a few, either don't flower

Indoor plants with soft, thin stems are unsuitable for rooting; outdoor plants that are dormant or entering dormancy are often difficult or impossible to root.

well or don't come true from seed, so rooting their cuttings is the most reliable way to propagate them.)

Some herbs were slower or less successful. Scented geraniums took twenty-six days to root vigorously; an Italian oregano took about as long, but the roots were weak and sparse. Fruit sage took nearly four weeks. Two lavender varieties I tried rooted in a little over six weeks, but only a small percentage of another struck roots, and weak ones at that.

A few of the herbs didn't

respond at all. French tarragon, thyme, balm of Gilead, and myrtle either rotted or had failed to root after two months. Two cultivars of common sage did not root at all. (All of these can be propagated by division or are fairly easy to root in a peat-based medium that is misted frequently.) I found that not all varieties of the same herb species rooted with the same speed or vigor, but this is also true with other propagation methods.

Some techniques that improve the rooting of cuttings in other media don't work when used with water. Scented geraniums, for instance, often root better when they are cut in the evening and allowed to sit in a plastic bag overnight to allow the wound to heal before they are stuck in a soilless medium. The cuttings that I treated this way did not root at all in water, while untreated ones did well. I knew that wounding cuttings of sweet bay by scraping either side of the stem helps them strike roots in a peat-perlite medium, but this didn't seem to make any difference in water.

The response of bay cuttings surprised me. Even under the most favorable conditions—with root-zone heating and intermittent misting—only 50 to 70 percent of my woody bay cuttings will root in a soilless growing medium after six to eight weeks. I tried them in water, and they just sat in their Styrofoam cups

without striking a single root. At the end of two months, the stems didn't appear callused, swollen, or ready to sprout roots, but the part of each stem that was under water was covered with wartlike nodes. I nearly gave up on them, but instead I moved them to 2½-inch pots containing my usual growing medium. Within a month, all were nicely rooted and growing well with no special care. A 100 percent success rate with bay cuttings was a first for me.

THE PROCEDURE

Although it's quite possible to throw a cutting in a glass of water and have it root, you're likely to have greater success with a wider range of cuttings if you pay attention to a few details. Take cuttings from plants that are in vigorous growth outdoors. Indoor plants with soft, thin stems are unsuitable for rooting; outdoor plants that are dormant or entering dormancy are often difficult or impossible to root. Generally, the best time for rooting cuttings is in spring, but I have had success with cuttings taken all through the growing season. Nonflowering stems are the best choice; remove any flower buds from other stems.

Choose plants that are free of disease and insects. As a hedge against failure, I like to cut several stems of each plant, putting them all in one container unless they seem overcrowded. Cut each stem about 3 to 4 inches from the tip with a sharp pair of scissors or knife and remove the lower leaves on the part that will be submerged. After your cuttings are ready, fill a glass, short jar, Styrofoam cup, or other container so that the bare stem is in water but the leaves stay dry; at least the top third of the cutting should extend above the container rim. I write the name of the variety and the date on each cup with a waterproof marker. Place the containers where they will receive plenty of bright light but no direct sun; I root my cuttings on the kitchen windowsill with a northern exposure.

Changing the water every day is the key to success with rooting in water. It keeps the water free from bacteria that can cause stems to rot.

As soon as the cuttings have roots 1/4 to 1/2 inch long, they are ready to transplant into pots; don't let them grow into a dense tangle. Cuttings rooted in water are transplanted the same way as seedlings except that a single stem is planted in each pot; the growing tip of the rooted cutting is cut right after transplanting to encourage branching. (See page 49 for transplanting tips.)

I have read so often that cuttings rooted in water do not transplant or grow well, but I have never had any problems as long as I first transplant them into a pot so that they can become estab-

lished plants, a system I also follow with cuttings rooted in a soilless mix.

Place the potted cuttings in a sunny window or a few inches below fluorescent lights or in a greenhouse. The heat in my greenhouse (often over 100°F during the day) made my summer cuttings grow quickly.

Rooting cuttings in water is a handy propagation technique for use throughout the growing season, but it is especially useful in late summer when it's time to start new plants to grow indoors over winter. With luck and a little attention, you'll have windowsills filled with rooted cuttings to enjoy during the cold months or to set out next spring, as well as some to share with friends.

ROOTING CUTTINGS IN A GROWING MEDIUM

My father-in-law, W.K. Doyle, delighted me one day with a story of how boxwood cuttings were rooted in the Shenandoah Valley of Virginia in the early part of this century. Nurserymen went door to door during the summer, asking permission to trim and shape the many boxwoods that adorned the dooryards of farms and houses in small towns. They performed the task free or for a low price, and took away gunny sacks filled with the clippings. They carried these to a nearby stream and stuck them in sandbars kept moist by the clear moun-

tain water. Nature took its course and in time the boxwoods rooted. Today, all sorts of high-tech equipment is available to accomplish the same task. An expensive machine on the market a few years ago made propagation as simple as plugging it into electric current and slipping a cutting in each slot; in a week or two the cutting was rooted. Both old and modern methods used to root cuttings have this in common: they create an environment that induces roots to form.

Time, moisture, light, and temperature play important and well-known roles in encouraging cuttings to root; other factors, such as oxygen, are less obvious to many gardeners. When there is plenty of oxygen, new roots are slender, branched, flexible, and easily transplanted; with limited oxygen there are fewer roots and those produced tend to be brittle and unbranched. The amount of oxygen available to cuttings is related to the rooting medium that is used.

A rooting medium should be free of diseases and weeds, hold water but drain well, and support cuttings upright; it also should be loose enough to be well aerated, and allow cuttings to be inserted easily without bending or injuring tender stems, which can prevent a cutting from rooting. A pH of around 6.5 will usually produce the most roots; one that is too acidic will slow or

Best Conditions for Rooting Cuttings

Rooting medium availing plenty of oxygen

Air temperature in the sixties

Root-zone temperature of 75–80°F

Frequent misting

12 to 14 hours of light per day

Feeding with water-soluble fertilizer

prevent root emergence.

A great variety of materials including sphagnum peat, perlite, vermiculite, sand, rockwool, and floral foam can be used to root cuttings. Though much used in the past, sand is rarely used today because it holds less moisture and air than do other popular media.

I favor a mixture of one part perlite and one part Pro-Mix BX, a commercial soilless growing medium that contains sphagnum peat moss, perlite, and vermiculite. I have used this mix successfully for years, but many commercial growers prefer other materials and are satisfied with them; some change their medium with the season or with the particular herb to be rooted. Perlite by itself may be a good choice in many climates during the low light and cool temperatures of winter because it provides good aeration and holds little water, which protects stems against rot, but its inability to hold water limits its use at other times of the year.

Cuttings root best when they have some leaves attached to them because the leaves produce chemicals that promote root initiation and growth; too many leaves, or very large leaves, on the other hand, speed water loss that can lead to wilting and quick death. Protecting the cutting from water loss and wilting by raising the humidity around the cuttings is most commonly achieved by misting the leaves

(which also cools the leaf surfaces). Mist may be applied automatically, or manually with a spray bottle each time you walk by your cuttings. Automatic mist systems that spray a fog of microscopic water particles are used in many commercial greenhouses.

Ambient air temperatures in the sixties and root-zone temperatures at 75° to 80°F are ideal for making cuttings root. For bottom heat, I use rubber heat mats plugged into a thermostat which is connected to a bulb thermometer stuck carefully into a flat of cuttings. For sunny summer days when the air temperature soars in my greenhouse, I drape a winter white polyethylene material with 70 percent opacity high over and around my propagation bench; it reduces temperatures around the cuttings and provides enough light for rooting.

Learning to grow herbs well on a commercial scale has been a long and sometimes painful process. In the early years, I remember showing a visiting grower my propagation area, a shelf under a bench in the greenhouse; I still remember her perplexed response: how can you root this stuff without light? I *was* able to root cuttings in the semi-dark under the bench (even an occasional bay cutting), but an awful lot of cuttings died. I purchased a cheap mist system, which improved

—continued on page 44

Simple Rooting
Environments

Here are some inexpensive ways to emulate professional rooting methods on a small scale.

🌾 In place of a propagation greenhouse with a fog system, construct a small polyethylene tent on a table near a window where there is bright light but no direct sun. Leave an opening on one end. Place pots containing cuttings inside the tent and aim a small room humidifier at the opening. Because natural light is almost always insufficient indoors, you could include fluorescent lights as the "roof" of the poly tent.

🌾 Make a container for rooting a few cuttings by folding an 8-by-24-inch polyethylene sheet in half lengthwise. Place a dampened mixture of equal parts of perlite and sphagnum peat in the fold. Stick prepared cuttings (see page 44) into the rooting medium and then carefully roll up the sheet, slip a rubber band around the roll, and place it upright in a humid, cool, shaded area so the sun will not cook the cuttings.

🌾 Place a pot of cuttings in a plastic bag. Stick two arches made from coat hanger or other flexible wire in the pot to support the top of the plastic bag so it won't touch the stem leaves. Place the pot in bright light but out of direct sun or the temperatures inside the bag will become lethal. Spritz the cuttings each day and then close the bag with a clothespin or twist tie; leave the bag open each night.

🌾 Maintaining enough humidity around cuttings to keep them from wilting is a major problem for the home gardener. Here's a way, adapted from a number of methods, that meets the challenge. Gather the fol-

In place of a propagation greenhouse with a fog system, construct a small polyethylene tent on a table near a window where there is bright light but no direct sun.

lowing: a six-inch plastic pot with its drainage holes plugged (florists' clay works well), a three-inch clay pot, enough dampened rooting medium to half fill the large pot. Scoop enough medium from the center of the large pot to fill the clay pot, then insert the clay pot up to its rim in the cavity. Stick cuttings in the clay pot and place the large pot under fluorescent lights with three inches between them and the large pot rim. Keep the medium damp around the small pot so it will humidify the air around the cuttings.

🌾 Several mail-order companies offer a plastic dome to hold humidity and a heat mat to maintain heat at the root zone. This combination is similar to what a professional grower might use on a larger scale.

my success, but I "saw the light" only when I realized that the short daylight hours of winter and early spring were hindering rooting. Installing overhead lights to extend short winter days led to quicker and firmer rooted cuttings. I now realize that light intensity and day length work together with root-zone heating and cool air temperatures to create the perfect rooting environment. The 12- to 14-hour

---

I pay little attention where I cut on the stem; above a node or leaf or below it doesn't seem to matter when it comes to making roots.

---

day is ideal for rooting cuttings, and as long as air temperatures are cool, the cuttings under mist stand tall. As air temperatures warm, I cut light levels (not day lengths) with shade cloth or white plastic to keep cuttings turgid.

Good gardeners recognize that it is important to supply nutrients to their plants, but this is not usually considered in the propagation of herb cuttings. Eli Putievsky, the Israeli researcher, discovered that small amounts of fertilizer applied every two days to sage

cuttings increased the number of cuttings that rooted from 79 percent to 90 percent. Of those that rooted, the fertilized cuttings averaged 128 percent more roots than the unfertilized ones. Fertilizing cuttings is worth trying with other herbs, too, but be careful not to soak the rooting medium. Root-zone heating, which helps to dry the rooting medium, is a must with this technique.

SELECTING AND PREPARING CUTTINGS

It takes a healthy stem cutting to produce a high quality plant. The best plants from which to take cuttings have been getting plenty of sun and are plump with vigorous, new, compact growth. Avoid plants that are wilted or appear stressed in any way, have yellow or moldy, brown leaves, or have spindly or weak branches. Stems that make the best cuttings are supple and strong but not woody. New growth—often referred to as soft-wood or herbaceous—is generally best for cuttings because it is most likely to root quickly and be disease- and insect-free. How to select the best stems to cut is hard to teach, because it is a visual and tactile skill amplified by intuition and experience.

Many guide books suggest using sharp razor knives to take cuttings. Perhaps I break too many rules, but I have always used scissors for all my herb cuttings (except for the

thick, woody stems of bay), and it hasn't hurt my rooting averages. Most herb stems are tender and succulent rather than thick and tough, so sharp scissors cut cleanly and make a nice wound which encourages the cells to multiply and make roots.

Selecting the best stems to cut takes some time, but it's important to work quickly so that the cuttings don't wilt before they can be stuck and put in an atmosphere of high humidity. I usually work in the early morning, but early evening might be even better with twelve hours of darkness to help the cuttings to adjust to their new status.

I try to cut stems to a uniform length, somewhere between 3 and 4 inches, but this varies with the herb variety and the condition of the stems on the mother plant. I pay little attention where I cut on the stem; above a node or leaf or below it doesn't seem to matter when it comes to making roots. The woodier and tougher part of the stem below this tip is slower to root, and the longer a cutting takes to root, the more danger it faces from disease. Disinfecting the cutting tool with alcohol after each cut will lessen the possibility of spreading disease from one plant to another.

The best time of year to take cuttings of most herbs is when plants are growing rapidly, daytime temperatures are still between 55° and 70°F, and nighttime temperatures are above freezing; cool weather is least stressful to cuttings. Stem tips cut during fall, when days are shorter and nighttime temperatures have dropped into the thirties, often root slowly because growth has been slowed by approaching dormancy. Fall is also the time when foliage diseases are most likely to be a problem where nighttime humidity is high.

The traditional way of propagating lavender and many other woody shrubs was to take dormant wood cuttings in the fall and stick them in open cold frames outdoors. These would root over winter and spring and then would be transplanted into the fields. Now, with mist systems and plastic pots to speed and ease the process, I've found that spring is a better time for taking cuttings. Cuttings taken from new spring growth of lavender root quickly and easily; this is the growth that will produce flowers, of course, and I remove the flower buds before I stick the cuttings.

Cuttings are extremely vulnerable once severed from the mother plant, and heat and strong sunlight can cause them to wilt quickly, so I move to a shady spot to prepare the cuttings for insertion into the rooting medium. I strip leaves from the lower half of the cuttings by quickly sliding my thumb and index finger down the stem. It takes some practice to get the pressure just right; the goal is for the leaves to come off without

A 3-inch stem tip of *Origanum vulgare* ssp. *hirtum* is an easy length to handle for rooting. Sharp scissors make a clean cut.

Strip the leaves off the lower half of the cutting by sliding thumb and index finger down the stem.

Dipping the stem in rooting hormone is beneficial to the rooting process, or the gardener's peace of mind, or both.

The cutting is stuck deeply into a pot or flat of loose soilless medium so that the leaves almost touch the surface of the medium.

—continued on page 47

PROPAGATING BAYS

Propagating cuttings of sweet bay (*Laurus nobilis*) takes some special techniques and patience. Bays recovering from a hard winter often grow continuously, and their stems do not harden sufficiently to make cuttings that will root successfully. Ordinarily, mature bays tend to grow in spurts with enough time for wood to stiffen to a snap break before a second flush of growth begins. The most promising material for

The factors that promoted the quickest and best roots under mist were wounding the stem and providing root-zone heat.

cuttings is half-hard stems that have lost the gloss of youth and tenderness, and are a bit middle-aged-stiff with a dull green hue. This stage

occurs near the time stem buds begin to swell with new energy.

A tough bay stem is easily crushed with scissors or regular pruners, but a razor-sharp utility knife will make a beautiful, clean cut; the knife will also come in handy for a later step in preparing the cutting for rooting. Remove the leaves from the lower part of the stem as for other cuttings, and then scrape opposite sides of the lower part of

To propagate a sweet bay, choose half-hard stems whose leaves have lost their tender, light green look.

Remove leaves from the lower half of the stem by stripping down the stem with your thumb and finger.

Scrape two opposite sides of the bare stem with a sharp utility knife to expose the white under-layer.

the green stem with the knife to expose the white under-layer. This allows more water to be absorbed by the cutting and also encourages the interior cells of the stem to begin division and root production.

For many years I used the strongest rooting hormone I could find in the belief that it would help tough-to-root bays, but when a grower acquaintance questioned this, I decided to test my assumption and found that indole-3-butryic acid, the active hormone in my rooting powder, actually hindered bay root development. The factors that promoted the quickest and best roots under mist were wounding the stem and providing root-zone heat. One-third more cuttings rooted with wounding, and root-zone heat cut rooting time by one-third. I've found that bay cuttings do well under mist, but they will also root if left in a cool, damp spot that is protected from drying breezes and direct sun.

damaging the stems. After the lower leaves are removed, I have a cutting that has a bare stem on the cut end and nice green leaves hugging the stem from the midpoint up to the growing tip. If I'm going to root these cuttings in water, I do it forthwith.

Before inserting the cuttings in rooting medium, I dip the bare part of the stem in rooting powder that contains less than 1 percent indole-3-butyric acid, a naturally occurring plant rooting hormone; this makes me feel better psychologically, but I don't know that it actually helps herbs to root. Most herbs root easily, and I've been less than systematic in evaluating the benefits of rooting powder on them, except for rosemary and bay cuttings. I've found that the roots on untreated rosemary cuttings tend to be less bushy than the roots from treated cuttings, but bay cuttings treated with hormones are less likely to root than untreated ones. Researchers can provide impressive photos to show the efficacy of applying rooting hormones, so I'll keep dipping my cuttings—just in case.

I've watched demonstrations of sticking cuttings and talked to growers about it, and I've come to the conclusion that with time you develop your own style of doing it. Many propagators use a dibble—a pointed stick about the size of a pencil—to punch a small hole in the soil or rooting medium so the rooting powder won't rub off when the cutting is stuck. I don't worry about this because even if it does rub off, the rooting hormone will still be around the rooting area. But dibbles are of value for seating thin or weak stems of herbs like thyme and oregano; when stuck into a dibbled hole, the stem won't bend or break, either of which would put an end to any chance of rooting.

I usually stick my herb cuttings in open plastic flats that measure 11 inches by 21 inches by $2^1/2$ inches deep; from 100 to 300 cuttings will fit in such a container, depending on the size of the cutting and the herb variety. Any sterile container that is no deeper than 2 or 3 inches may be used to root cuttings: pots, cell packs, or plug trays with tiny cells made to hold a single cutting each. I try to make the best use of my valuable greenhouse space, so I tend to keep cuttings close together; pots take up the most space.

I space cuttings far enough apart that their leaves don't quite touch; this permits some air to circulate through them, which lessens the likelihood

I space cuttings far enough apart that their leaves don't quite touch; this permits some air to circulate through them . . .

of disease in the super-humid propagation atmosphere. Pots that are at least 2 inches deep are useful for rooting just a few cuttings; those deeper than 3 inches may keep the rooting medium too wet, preventing proper aeration.

After the cuttings are all stuck in the flat, cellpack, plug tray, or pot, I water them with a gentle flow from a hose fitted with a water breaker; the water gently settles the rooting medium around the base of the cuttings without packing it. After the cuttings are firmed by the water, they go into the high-humidity envi-

ronment described on page 43.

TENDING THE CUTTINGS

In the cool, humid propagation area and the darkness of the rooting medium, some cuttings will inevitably die. On my daily check of my greenhouse propagation area, I remove any cuttings that are dead, because these will become vectors for disease that can spread rapidly to the other cuttings in the dampness. I check the rooting medium to make sure it is still moist; if it has begun to dry out, I water and fertilize it at the same time.

My ideal is that the mist will barely have dried on the leaf surfaces of my cuttings before the next burst of moisture falls—a difficult condition to maintain when you're misting by hand. Some propagators feel that it is beneficial to allow the cuttings to wilt moderately between waterings; they believe that this stress stimulates the cutting to root and makes a tougher plant. I belong to the school that believes in pampering cuttings, not stressing them. I do everything I can to prevent the cuttings from wilting, including misting frequently and hanging shade cloth or white poly over the propagation area during hot weather.

After the first week, I get anxious and begin to check the progress of my cuttings; I tug cuttings at random to see if there is any resistance caused by new roots. I remove a cut-

ting or two, looking for a callus, an ugly mass of cells that swells the stem and eventually cracks with roots. I'm elated when I find cuttings with roots; I know that I've been successful at working with nature again. Soon I'll see top growth (though sometimes it starts even before roots form).

When the roots are from 1/4 to 1/2 inch long, the cuttings are ready to transplant, and I remove them from their pampered rooting environment. A delay of a day or two in moving cuttings from the humid propagation area can sometimes be all that is needed for disease to sweep through. Sometimes I leave the flats on heat mats to encourage roots to continue developing rapidly, or if roots are vigorous, I put the flats on a sunny bench in the greenhouse for a few days before transplanting the cuttings to

Cuttings can be stuck two or three to a pot with their leaves just touching but with plenty of room for air circulation.

This oregano cutting has struck roots after a week to ten days, but is not yet ready to transplant. Note that the rooting medium still clings to the stem.

Pruning an oregano as soon as it's transplanted to its growing pot will help it branch and get bushy.

Knock rooted cuttings from their pots to see if they're ready to transplant to the garden. Enough roots should show around the edges to hold the growing medium together.

2½-inch pots.

TRANSPLANTING ROOTED CUTTINGS

I transplant rooted cuttings into pots filled with my favorite peatlite mix, handling them much as I do seedlings (see pages 30–32), with a few exceptions. I still use my finger as a dibble, but I put a single cutting instead of a clump into each hole. I cut the growing tip of each cutting to encourage it to branch at the same time that it is filling the pot with roots; with most herb varieties, this produces a nice branched plant in a few weeks. As I move the rooted cuttings from the flat to pots, I try to keep as much of the rooting medium with the roots as pos-sible. My goal is to have an empty flat when all the cuttings are transplanted.

After a cutting has been transplanted and pruned, it is on its own to grow in the sun (or under fluorescent lights); it gets fertilizer once a week and water as needed. To see whether a new plant is ready to transplant to the garden, I knock it gently from the pot to check root development; I want to see enough roots at the edge of the root ball to hold the growing medium together. At the other end of the plant I want to see enough foliage to cover the top of the growing medium and reach the edge of the pot. I transplant rooted cuttings into the garden in the same way that I do seedlings (pages 30–32).

Many years ago, in the quiet time before my hobby got out of hand and turned into a business, I would look at my herb garden and see delightful shapes and smell rich fragrances, and dream of ways to use them. My professional experiences in growing new plants vegetatively has changed my perspective. When I look at my herb garden today, I see the potential for making new plants from branches, crowns, and roots. The propagation game is so challenging and productive that I would encourage even the greenest herb neophyte to try making the kindest cut, the separation that creates new life.

TRANSPLANTING
AND THE FIRST YEAR

When herbs are ready to transfer to the garden, outdoor temperatures should be appropriate for the species so that continuous growth is maintained; a setback caused by cold could seriously slow development or be fatal to sensitive plants. Some herbs such as chervil, parsley, and sor-

I favor soil that is well worked and so full of humus that using a trowel or a large dibble is unnecessary; just a hand will do fine, thank you.

rel grow best in cool weather; others such as basil need nearly tropical temperatures for best growth. With careful planning, you can avoid having plants ready to transplant at a time when inhospitable weather rules the garden.

The planning for transplant day needs to begin months before you sow the first seed or take the first cutting. Getting the timing right is tough because even within a single state there can be a wide range of weather conditions; temperatures may vary as much five to ten degrees in two places on a 50 by 100 foot lot, if my yard is any gauge. After you've gardened in the same spot for a number of years, experience and intuition will become reliable guides; until then, the accompanying charts may be a helpful planning tool.

Determining when to sow seed so that transplants will be ready at the proper time (if the weather plays no tricks) is as easy as counting the days on a calendar. Find the herb you plan to propagate on the appropriate chart (page 62) and note the number of days it takes from seed to transplant. Look up the appropriate transplant temperature for that herb on the chart. For instance, lemon balm should be transplanted when nighttime temperatures are 50°F.

This would be sometime after growers in your area transplant cabbage and before they transplant tomatoes. Now take a calender and mark the transplant date and count backward the number of days from sow to transplant; this is the seeding day or day to stick cuttings. Weather is always uncertain but you'll have a couple of weeks of slack if Nature tricks you. If your seedlings start to become overgrown during a wait, take a pair of scissors and snip some stems to enjoy while you wait for the bad weather to break. Timing when to take cuttings is less certain because it's harder to control when roots will appear. Time and experience will help you learn to gauge this.

INTO THE GARDEN

This isn't a book about garden planning, so I'll simply advise you to place the herbs carefully in the design that makes you happy, allowing room for air currents around them when they reach maturity. I favor soil that is well worked and so full of humus

Well-prepared soil is so loose you can dig it with your hand. Some well rotted manure or a few beads of slow-release fertilizer will help the plant get off to a good start.

To transplant a hardened-off oregano to the garden, first amend and dig the soil deeply, then gently knock the plant from its pot.

Spread the roots by gently tearing and spreading the base of the root ball. Insert plant slightly deeper than it was growing in the pot. A shallow depressions around the plant will channel moisture to the roots.

that using a trowel or a large dibble is unnecessary; just a hand will do fine, thank you. I carefully knock the plant from its pot (never pulling it out by the stem, which might rip it from its roots), spread the roots by tearing them a bit at the bottom of the root ball if they are circling it, and then place the plant in a hole slightly lower than it was growing in the pot. I might throw a little composted manure or a few beads of slow-release fertilizer in the hole with the roots; added nutrients usually depend on the general level of soil fertility. If the stems are long enough, I prune them after transplanting to give the plant a little shape and start the stems branching. When I water a new plant for

the first time right after transplanting it, I use a liquid fertilizer instead of plain water.

EXPLAINING THE CHARTS

A few words about the charts (pages 56–67) may provide some interpretive assistance. There are many things a gardener wants to know about herbs other than their aroma and which variety is "best". Charts, for all their ability to convey information with precision and brevity, omit nuances on which good gardening depends. The column that lists the light requirement for acceptable growth, for instance, makes many compromises. The sun does not provide rays of light of equal intensity each hour, and so it is best to use the

numbers as a guide and evaluate the outcome by the growth of the herbs; if growth does not reach your expectations, you probably need a sunnier location.

Spacing herb plants is an inexact art, but it is important to their health and vigor. Plants grow differently in response to climatic conditions, but pruning can make a rambler or a sprawler dress up and conform to a more confined existence. The spacing dimensions should be taken as guides, not absolutes.

The hardiness of herbs (and other plants) is every bit as inexact as spacing, and the numbers on my chart reflect this. There are so many variables with weather that killing temperatures may vary by 20 degrees or more, because cold winter winds rob dormant plants of irreplaceable life-sustaining moisture. The temperatures I've listed, however inexact they may be, are for plants in the ground, not potted ones whose roots are less protected. Often, predicting hardiness is just a good guess; it's prudent to prepare for and expect the worst.

The charts show my personal preferences for covering seed for germination. Covering seeds started indoors is less critical because moisture is more easily regulated. On the other hand, light will pene-

---

Hand weeding around herbs has its aromatic pleasures, and it will always be welcome and necessary.

---

trate the little growing medium used as a cover and reach seeds needing it.

It would be impossible to provide an exact date on which it would be safe to transplant a particular herb into a garden and make it accurate across the U.S.; this explains why I have chosen to list air temperatures at night and relate planting dates to popular vegetables; weather is fickle and it is important to be

conservative when dealing with it and important plants.

THE FIRST YEAR

The first—and only—year of an annual herb has a lot crammed into it: birth, youth, old age, and death. For an annual, "life" is a four-letter word. The first year for the normally slower-growing perennial herb is one of dependence and struggle to become established; during this year you can do much to guide the plant toward future health and vigor. The following advice is generally good for annuals and perennials.

Monitor plants regularly and make certain they do not wilt from lack of water during summer's heat. Good gardeners get that way because they have observed their plants carefully over many years. Regular examination of your plants can help you identify problems as they begin when it is easier to combat them.

Pinch or cut stem tips regularly to encourage branching; this pruning strengthens stems and creates more foliage, both characteristics that help build plant health and vigor. Careful pruning of woody perennials for shape during this first year can set the pattern for the plant in years to come.

Fertilize fortnightly with liquid nutrients. Contrary to some conventional advice, feeding your herbs will not change or diminish their aroma; though they may be able to survive between a rock

and a hard place in the wild—and in your garden—they will reward generous feeding with bountiful harvests. In the second and succeeding years, a single application of fertilizer or organic nutrients at the beginning of the growing season should be sufficient for perennials; fast-growing annuals and biennials used for their leaves such as basil, parsley, coriander, dill, and chervil benefit from fortnightly feedings.

Fungus diseases may attack young plants during damp, cloudy, warm weather. Diseases make themselves known when foliage begins to turn yellow and die, and when the plant wilts for no apparent reason. Herbs with dense foliage or weak stems that touch the ground are vulnerable to diseases that prey on foliage hidden from light or near the ground; keep low-lying stems pruned and check areas of the plant that receive reduced light so that when a problem arises you find it when it is small and excise it. Avoid excessive watering from above, which keeps foliage wetter than it should be. Improve air circulation around herbs by pruning to open up the interior of the plants.

Most herbs don't compete well with weeds. Traditional mulches of organic matter aren't a good guard against weeds because they tend to foster diseases on plants whose foliage rests on or near the ground. Hand weeding around herbs has its aromatic pleasures, and it will always be welcome and necessary. A 1-inch-thick mulch of sand or light-colored gravel helps smother weeds and also reflects drying heat into the interior of dense plants, controlling diseases spread by moisture.

Night-feeding slugs can be problems all season long, but they are particularly active during cool, damp weather. Spring transplants and young seedlings are vulnerable to these slimy creatures' voracious appetites. Saucers of beer, broken eggshells, midnight searches with flashlights, and diatomaceous earth are all recommended slug deterrents.

However, nothing works better to keep slugs away than thin sheets of four-inch wide copper. Garden centers and mail-order firms sell copper for this purpose and copper flashing is available at roofing supply stores. Stand the copper upright, press it into the ground far enough so that it will stand up and fence in the garden bed or plants to be protected; of course, make sure no slugs are under mulch or elsewhere inside the copper fence. As elsewhere in life and art, success often teeters on achieving a balance of opposites, and in the garden, you want the balance to tip in your favor without having to set off atom bombs.

In the first year, keep patient and remember that failure is an invitation to learn more about yourself and the plants you cultivate. As Charles Dudley Warner saw it in his wise and humorous book, My *Summer in a Garden:* "The most humiliating thing to me about a garden is the lesson it teaches of the inferiority of man. Nature is prompt, decided, inexhaustible. She thrusts up her plants with a vigor and freedom that I admire; and the more worthless the plant, the more rapid and splendid its growth."

USEFUL
INFORMATION

GENERAL INFORMATION FOR SOME COMMON HERBS

Common Name Botanical Name	Life Span	Propagation
ANGELICA *Angelica archangelica*	Biennial	seed
ANISE HYSSOP *Agastache foeniculum*	Perennial	seed
BASIL *Ocimum basilicum*	Annual	seed, cutting
BAY *Laurus nobilis*	Perennial	cutting, seed division
BEE BALM *Monarda* species	Perennial	cutting, division
BORAGE *Borago officinalis*	Annual	seed
BURNET *Poterium sanguisorba*	Perennial	seed
CATNIP *Nepeta cataria*	Perennial	cutting, seed, division
CHAMOMILE, GERMAN *Matricaria recutita*	Annual	seed
CHAMOMILE, ROMAN *Chamaemelum nobile*	Perennial	seed, layering
CHERVIL *Anthriscus cerefolium*	Annual	seed
CHIVES *Allium shoenoprasum*	Perennial	seed, division
COMFREY *Symphytum* species	Perennial	seed, division
CORIANDER (CILANTRO) *Coriandrum sativum*	Annual	seed
COSTMARY *Tanacetum balsamita*	Perennial	cutting, division
CURRY PLANT *Helichrysum italicum*	Perennial	cutting
DILL *Anethum graveolens*	Annual	seed
FENNEL *Foeniculum vulgare*	Perennial	seed, division

Light Requirement	Hardy To	Mature Height	Spacing
part sun	−35°F	60"	36"
part/full sun	−20°F	36"	12"
full sun	35°F	24"	18"
part/full sun	15°F	480"	n.a.
shade/part/full sun	−20°F	36"	12"
full sun	30°F	24"	12"
part/full sun	−40°F	36"	18"
part/full sun	−40°F	36"	18"
part/full sun	32°F	30"	18"
part/full sun	−40°F	12"	6"
part sun	20°F	24"	9"
full sun	−40°F	18"	12"
part/full sun	−40°F	60"	36"
part/full sun	25°F	36"	12"
part/full sun	−20°F	36"	24"
full sun	10°F	18"	12"
full sun	29°F	36"	12"
full sun	−10°F	48"–60"	15"

GENERAL INFORMATION FOR SOME COMMON HERBS

Common Name Botanical Name	Life Span	Propagation
FEVERFEW *Tanacetum parthenium*	Perennial	seed, cutting
GERANIUM, SCENTED *Pelargonium* species	Perennial	cutting, seed
HYSSOP *Hyssopus officinalis*	Perennial	seed, cutting
LADY'S MANTLE *Alchemilla vulgaris*	Perennial	division
LAMBS' EARS *Stachys byzantina*	Perennial	division, seed
LAVANDIN *Lavandula × intermedia*	Perennial	cutting, layering
LAVENDER, ENGLISH *Lavandula angustifolia*	Perennial	layering, cutting, seed
LAVENDER, FRINGED *Lavandula dentata*	Perennial	cutting, layering
LAVENDER, SPANISH *Lavandula stoechas*	Perennial	cutting, layering
LEMON BALM *Melissa officinalis*	Perennial	seed, cutting, division
LEMON VERBENA *Aloysia triphylla*	Perennial	cutting, layering
LOVAGE *Levisticum officinale*	Perennial	seed, division
MARJORAM *Origanum majorana*	Perennial	seed, cutting
MINT *Mentha* species	Perennial	cutting, division
MEXICAN MINT MARIGOLD *Tagetes lucida*	Perennial	seed, cutting, layering
MYRTLE *Myrtus communis*	Perennial	cutting, layering
OREGANO *Origanum vulgare* ssp. *hirtum*	Perennial	seed, cutting, layering division
PARSLEY *Petroselinum crispum*	Biennial	seed

Light Requirement	Hardy To	Mature Height	Spacing
part/full sun	0°F	36"	18"
full sun	25°F	30"	20"
part/full sun	−20°F	24"	24"
part/full sun	−35°F	18"	12"
full sun	−35°F	18"	18"
full sun	0°F	30"–48"	24"
full sun	0°F	30"	24"
full sun	20°F	24"–30"	18"
full sun	15°F	24"–30"	18"
shade/part/full sun	−20°F	24"	18"
full sun	25°F	60"	36"
part/full sun	−35°F	72"	36"
full sun	20°F	12"	10"
part/full sun	−20°F	24"	15"
part shade/full sun	15°F	18"	10"
part/full sun	26°F	72"	48"
full sun	−20°F	24"	12"
part/full sun	15°F	18"	12"

GENERAL INFORMATION FOR SOME COMMON HERBS

Common Name Botanical Name	Life Span	Propagation
ROSEMARY *Rosmarinus officinalis*	Perennial	cutting, layering
RUE *Ruta graveolens*	Perennial	seed, cutting, layering
SAGE *Salvia officinalis*	Perennial	seed, cutting, layering
SANTOLINA *Santolina* species	Perennial	seed, cutting, layering
SAVORY, SUMMER *Satureja hortensis*	Annual	seed, cutting
SAVORY, WINTER *Satureja montana*	Perennial	seed, cutting, layering
SORREL *Rumex acetosa*	Perennial	seed, division
SOUTHERNWOOD *Artemisia abrotanum*	Perennial	cutting, division, layering
TANSY *Tanacetum vulgare*	Perennial	seed, cutting, division
TARRAGON, FRENCH *Artemisia dracunculus* var. *sativa*	Perennial	cutting, division
THYME, ENGLISH *Thymus* 'Broad-leaf English'	Perennial	cutting, layering
THYME, FRENCH *Thymus vulgaris* 'Narrow-leaf French'	Perennial	seed, cutting, layering, division
WOODRUFF *Galium odoratum*	Perennial	cutting, division
WORMWOOD *Artemisia absinthium*	Perennial	seed, division
YARROW *Achillea* species	Perennial	seed, division

Light Requirement	Hardy To	Mature Height	Spacing
part/full sun	10°–15°F	48–72"	36"
full sun	−20°F	36"	18"
full sun	−20°–10°F	30"	24"
part/full sun	−5°F	24"	18"
full sun	33°F	18"	12"
full sun	−10°F	18"	12"
part/full sun	−20°F	18"	12"
full sun	−20°F	48"	36"
part/full sun	−20°F	48"	24"
full sun	−20°F	24"	24"
part/full sun	−20°F	12"	18"
part/full sun	−20°F	16"	18"
shade	−35°F	8"	9"
part/full sun	−20°F	50"	36"
full sun	−50°F	36"	24"

HERBS COMMONLY GROWN FROM SEED

Common Name Botanical Name	Seeds per Ounce	Viability[1]	Cover/ Uncover
ANISE HYSSOP *Agastache foeniculum*	70,000	70%	uncovered
BASIL, SWEET *Ocimum basilicum*	17,750	60%	uncovered
BORAGE *Borago officinalis*	1,600	70%	covered
CATNIP *Nepeta cataria*	41,000	40%	uncovered
CHAMOMILE, GERMAN *Matricaria recutita*	275,000	40%	uncovered
CHERVIL *Anthriscus cerefolium*	10,000	65%	covered
CHIVES *Allium schoenoprasum*	22,000	50%	covered
CORIANDER (CILANTRO) *Coriandrum sativum*	1,700	70%	covered
DILL *Anethum graveolens*	21,800	60%	covered
FENNEL *Foeniculum vulgare*	8,000	80%	covered
FEVERFEW *Tanacetum*	145,000	60%	uncovered
LEMON BALM *Melissa officinalis*	50,000	60%	covered
LOVAGE *Levisticum officinale*	8,000	50%	covered
MARJORAM *Origanum majorana*	165,000	50%	uncovered
OREGANO *Origanum vulgare*	354,000	50%	uncovered

[1] Average viability based on data from Park Seed Co., Johnny's Selected Seed, and interviews with herb growers.
[2] Production times are for optimum indoor conditions. Seedlings are clump transplanted.
[3] Plants should be hardened off for about a week before being planted in the garden (see page 33).
[4] Transplanting temperatures are estimates based on average nighttime lows and are related to transplanting common vegetables as follows: broccoli or cabbage, 45°F; tomato or pepper, 55°F; eggplant, 60°F.

Germination Time at 70°[2]	Germination to Potting Up	Potting Up to Garden[3]	Nighttime Temperature at Transplant[4]
6 days	20 days	14 days	55°F
4 days	18 days	14 days	65°F
5 days	15 days	11 days	55°F
5 days	25 days	14 days	50°F
4 days	20 days	14 days	45°F
7 days	10 days	12 days	45°F
6 days	direct seeded	25 days	45°F
6 days	13 days	10 days	50°F
5 days	11 days	16 days	50°F
6 days	14 days	20 days	50°F
5 days	20 days	24 days	55°F
7 days	21 days	15 days	50°F
8 days	21 days	12 days	45°F
5 days	12 days	14 days	55°F
4 days	30 days	14 days	50°F

HERBS COMMONLY GROWN FROM SEED

Common Name Botanical Name	Seeds per Ounce	Viability[1]	Cover/ Uncover
PARSLEY *Petroselinum crispum*	15,000	60%	covered
SAGE *Salvia officinalis*	3,400	60%	covered
SAVORY, SUMMER *Satureja hortensis*	47,500	55%	uncovered
SAVORY, WINTER *Satureja montana*	49,700	55%	uncovered
SORREL *Rumex acetosa*	33,000	65%	uncovered
THYME, FRENCH *Thymus vulgaris,* 'Narrow-leaf French'	98,200	50%	uncovered
WORMWOOD *Artemisia absinthium*	191,400	30%	uncovered

[1]Average viability based on data from Park Seed Co., Johnny's Selected Seed, and interviews with herb growers.
[2]Production times are for optimum indoor conditions. Seedlings are clump transplanted.
[3]Plants should be hardened off for about a week before being planted in the garden (see page 33).
[4]Transplanting temperatures are estimates based on average nighttime lows and are related to transplanting common vegetables as follows: broccoli or cabbage, 45°F; tomato or pepper, 55°F; eggplant, 60°F.

Germination Time at 70°[2]	Germination to Potting Up	Potting Up to Garden[3]	Nighttime Temperature at Transplant[4]
8 days	12 days	14 days	50°F
9 days	17 days	14 days	55°F
6 days	21 days	19 days	55°F
5 days	30 days	24 days	55°F
2 days	14 days	14 days	45°F
4 days	21 days	19 days	50°F
5 days	25 days	14 days	50°F

HERBS COMMONLY GROWN FROM CUTTINGS

Common Name Botanical Name	Production Time[1]	Nighttime Temperature at Tramsplant[2]	Comments
BAY *Laurus nobilis*	60–100 days	55°F	Usually grown as pot plant.
BEE BALM *Monarda* species	38 days	55°F	Mildew can be a problem on foliage.
CATNIP *Nepeta cataria*	40 days	50°F	Roots quickly.
CHAMOMILE, ROMAN *Chamaemelum nobile*	35 days	55°F	2½ -inch cuttings work fine.
CURRY PLANT *Helichrysum italicum*	55 days	50°F	Gray, hairy leaves are fungus prone; cuttings need less mist or humidity.
FEVERFEW *Tanacetum parthenium*	40 days	55°F	Especially useful way to save showy flowering varieties.
GERANIUM, SCENTED *Pelargonium* species	45 days	55°F	Allow cutting wound to "heal" overnight by placing it in a plastic bag kept in a cool place. Not all varieties root eagerly.
HYSSOP *Hyssopus officinalis*	42 days	50°F	Best way to propagate white and pink-flowered varieties.
LAVENDER *Lavandula* species	50 days	55°F	Vegetative propagation is a must for named varieties.
LEMON BALM *Melissa officinalis*	30 days	50°F	Easy method when divisions are not possible.
LEMON VERBENA *Aloysia triphylla*	40 days	55°F	Guard against mites and white flies on cutting material.
MARJORAM *Origanum majorana*	35 days	55°F	Cuttings less likely to develop stem rot.
MINT *Mentha* species	27 days	55°F	Roots easily in water.
OREGANO *Origanum vulgare* ssp. *hirtum*	35 days	55°F	Easily rooted and quick to branch

[1]Production times are for optimum indoor conditions with root-zone heating and intermittent mist. Production time is measured from the day cuttings are stuck until transplants are garden ready.

[2]Transplanting temperatures are estimates based on average nighttime lows and are related to transplanting common vegetables as follows: broccoli or cabbage, 45°F; tomato or pepper, 55°F; eggplant, 60°F.

Common Name Botanical Name	Production Time[1]	Nighttime Temperature at Tramsplant[2]	Comments
ROSEMARY *Rosmarinus officinalis*	49 days	55°F	Light-colored, greenish stems root quickly.
RUE *Ruta graveolens*	53 days	55°F	Propagate handsome named varieties vegetatively. Spring growth roots quickly.
SAGE *Salvia officinalis*	45 days	55°F	Spring cuttings easiest to root. Best way to produce named varieties with colorful leaves.
SANTOLINA *Santolina* species	60 days	55°F	Drier rooting conditions protect against disease.
SAVORY, WINTER *Satureja montana*	50 days	55°F	Less stem rot problems from cuttings; a good way to preserve variations in flower color.
SOUTHERNWOOD *Artemisia abrotanum*	65 days	55°F	Seeds not available of this lovely scented herb. Choose new spring growth for easiest rooting.
TARRAGON, FRENCH *Artemisia dracunculus*	50 days	55°F	Early spring growth roots best. Highly susceptible to fungus.
THYME, ENGLISH *Thumus* 'Broad-leaf English'	50 days	50°F	Tender new growth roots quickly; avoid stems in flower.

CREATING YOUR OWN SOILLESS GROWING MEDIUM

French gardeners experimented before 1892 with growing media that did not contain mineral soil. They successfully grew azaleas in a combination of peat, leafmold, and pine needles. After World War II, U.S. horticulturists, spurred by dwindling topsoil resources, developed soilless media for the plant growing industry.

Most of the commercially available soilless media are based on formulas developed at Cornell University in the late 1950s. They are comprised of sphagnum peat moss, composted bark or peanut hulls, perlite, and vermiculite. Because these substances contain few nutrients, plants grown in them require the frequent application of fertilizers. Earlier formulas created at the University of California also used peat moss, but the aggregate of choice was fine sand.

Kenneth F. Baker, who was instrumental in developing the media, favored fine sand because he said it made his mix approach "loam in water and nutrient retention". He also advocated the use of some organic sources of nitrogen because the nutrient was released slowly over an extended period of time.

Over the years, I have found that available brands of soilless media grow healthy, vigorous herbs without the additional problems of weediness and disease associated with soil-based mixes, but regular fertilization is important (fish emulsion works well). Large quantities of growing media purchased at retail prices may break your budget. Gardeners have a reputation for self-reliance and do-it-yourself innovation; many actually shrink from the idea of buying something they can make themselves.

For a quick all-purpose soilless mix, you may find that equal parts of dry sphagnum peat and perlite will work well as a starter. To each gallon of this mix, add a handful of Osmocote For Potting Mixes (the 17-6-10 slow release formula contains the necessary trace elements that are missing from the soilless mix), and a heaping tablespoon of ground limestone. Dampen with warm water—using a hard spray that roughs the mix or kneading the mix energetically with your hands helps the peat take up the water—and it's ready to use. Don't store dampened mix for prolonged periods. This quick recipe comes closest to the popular Cornell mix B which drains well, a characteristic favored for herbs.

RESOURCES

I sell no seed and don't ship plants. There are hundreds of small enterprises like mine in the U.S. and I encourage you to patronize these local establishments; personal contact with herb plants and those who grow them is the best way to determine an herb's suitability for the garden and your kitchen. Everybody isn't fortunate enough to have local resources, but there are many mailorder companies that provide hard-to-find seeds and plants. Only a small selection is listed here.

Extensive lists of mailorder and local herb farms can be found in Bobbi A. McRae's *The Herb Companion Wishbook and Resource Guide* (Interweave Press, 201 East Fourth Street, Loveland, Colorado 80537) and in Paula Oliver's *The Herb Gardener's Resource Guide* (Northwind Farm, Rt. 2, Box 246, Shevlin, Minnesota 56676). Those readers interested in broadening their herbal educations through correspondence and on-site classes will find these listed in Laura Z. Clavio's *Directory of Herbal Education* (Intra-American Specialties, 3014 N 400 West, West Lafayette, Indiana 47906).

Herb seeds and plants

Nichols Garden Nursery
1190 N. Pacific Highway
Albany, OR 97321
(503) 928-9280. Catalog, free.

Flowery Branch Seed Co.
PO Box 1330
Flowery Branch, GA 30542
(404) 536-8380. Catalog, $3.

Companion Plants
7247 N. Coolville Ridge Rd.
Athens, OH 45701
(614) 592-4643. Catalog, $3.

Lewis Mtn. Herbs & Everlastings
2345 St. Rt. 247
Manchester, OH 45144
(513) 549-2484. Catalog, $1.

Rasland Farm
Rt. 1, Box 65, NC 82 at US 13
Godwin, NC 28344
(910) 567-2705. Catalog, $2.50.

Redwood City Seed Co.
PO Box 361
Redwood City, CA 94064
(415) 325-7333. Catalog, $1.

Richters
PO Box 26
Goodwood, Ontario L0C 1A0, Canada
(905) 640-6677. Catalog, $2.

Sandy Mush Herb Nursery
316 Surrett Cove Rd.
Leicester, NC 28748
(704) 683-2014. Catalog, $4.

The Herbfarm
32804 Issaquah-Fall City Rd.
Fall City, WA 98024
(800) 866-4372. Master plant list, $3.50.

Well-Sweep Herb Farm
317 Mt. Bethel Rd.
Port Murray, NJ 07865
(908) 852-5390. Catalog, $2.

Goodwin Creek Gardens
PO Box 83
Williams, OR 97544
(503) 846-7357. Catalog, $1.

Seeds and supplies

Johnny's Selected Seeds
Foss Hill Rd.
Albion, ME 04910
(207) 437-4301. Catalog, free.

Park Seed Company
Cokesbury Rd.
Greenwood, SC 29647
(800) 845-3366. The firm's wholesale division has misting equipment and other propagation supplies used by commercial growers. Catalog, free.

W. Atlee Burpee & Company
Warminster, PA 18974
(215) 674-1793. Catalog, free.

Scented geraniums

Davidson-Wilson Greenhouses
R.R. 2, Box 168
Crawfordsville, IN 47933
(317) 364-0556. Catalog, $3.

Supplies

Gardener's Supply Company
128 Intervale Rd.
Burlington, VT 05401
(800) 444-6417. Catalog, free.

A.M. Leonard, Inc.
PO Box 816
Piqua, OH 45356
(800) 543-8955. Catalog, free.

INDEX